BLUE &
WHITE
LIVING

BLUE & WHITE
LIVING

STEPHANIE HOPPEN
FRITZ VON DER SCHULENBURG

CLARKSON POTTER/PUBLISHERS
NEW YORK

Text copyright © 1998 Stephanie Hoppen and Fritz von der Schulenburg
Photographs copyright © 1998 Fritz von der Schulenburg

Published by Clarkson N. Potter/Publishers, 201 East 50th Street,
New York, New York 10022.
Member of the Crown Publishing Group.

Random House, Inc. New York, Toronto, London, Sydney, Auckland
www.randomhouse.com

CLARKSON N. POTTER, POTTER, and colophon are trademarks of
Clarkson N. Potter, Inc.

Originally published in the United Kingdom by Collins & Brown Limited,
London House, Great Eastern Wharf, Parkgate Road, London,
SW11 4NQ in 1998.

Printed in Hong Kong

Designer: David Fordham
Photographer: Fritz von der Schulenburg

Library of Congress Cataloging-in-Publication Data
Hoppen, Stephanie.
    Blue and white living / Stephanie Hoppen : photographs by Fritz
von der Schulenburg.
        p.   cm.
    "First published in the United Kingdom in 1998 by Collins &
Brown" —T. p. verso.
        Includes index.
        1. Interior decoration.   2. Blue in interior decoration.   3. White
in interior decoration.   I. Von der Schulenburg, Fritz.   II. Title.
NK2115.5.C6H663 1998
747'.94—dc21   98-26051
                                                              CIP

ISBN 0-609-60356-6

10 9 8 7 6 5 4 3 2

Contents

7   Foreword by Patrick Frey of Pierre Frey

8   My Life in Blue & White

13   One: The World of Blue & White

33   Two: Living in Blue & White

57   Three: Dining in Blue & White

77   Four: Sleeping in Blue & White

99   Five: Bathing in Blue & White

113   Six: Blue & White Collections

137   Seven: Blue & White Fabrics

145   Eight: Blue & White Pictures

156   Suppliers

160   Index

LEFT Shades and tones of blue and white are reflected as much in nature as they are in design, illustrated here in the turquoise waters of the Maldives and the azure blue of a swimming pool, the deep blues of the ocean, and the hazy blue of the skies above Toronto and La Grande Montee.

BLUE, THE COLOR OF EYES, THE SKY, THE SEA and of heaven, is probably everybody's favorite color. It is also the only color whose shades can be mixed together with an invariably happy result. Blue also co-ordinates beautifully with other colors – blue and white, blue and red, blue and yellow. In fact, it is one of the most popular colors used in our daily lives – "Blue de Nimes" or blue denim is a universal favorite. China plates and crockery, bed and table linen, furnishing fabrics, wallpaper, and Portuguese "Azurelos" tiles have all favored blue, whatever the age or style.

Blue represents elegance, simplicity, and tranquility. What other color commands such enthusiasm, and for so long? In the art world, what painter has not had a "blue" period – Picasso and Matisse are two of many. The greatest interior designers, past, present and to come, never tire of using blue, and all of them, at one time or another, have wanted to design a blue and white room. Blue has always featured in our own collection of furnishing fabrics. It is a timeless color which can be used to great effect in *camaieu* (monochrome) or in combination with another color.

This book is a wonderful idea and throughout these pages, you will discover a multitude of shades, uses and locations that Stephanie Hoppen has chosen or created with such great talent and we will always be grateful to her for having written this book. It is a beautiful testament to blue and white and will always be studied with pleasure.

Patrick Frey

MY LIFE IN BLUE & WHITE

Although I have always loved blue and white as a color combination, I don't think I had any conception of how wonderful it was until about twelve years ago when I bought an enchanting house in Chelsea, London. The dining room of my late eighteenth-century home was to display all my blue and white china.

Over a period of one year, a rather special room evolved: the blue dining room that has appeared in almost every home magazine and book about dining rooms in the Western world. The centerpiece of the dining room is a marvelous 17th-century Dutch china cabinet. Its exterior is almost a silver white with shelves painted in a faded, distressed blue, signaling its aristocratic heritage. It was evidently meant to store and display all the porcelain and ceramics that would have been essential to any Dutch household. Before the cabinet was delivered, we painted and dragged the walls in the same blue as the cupboard shelves. When it arrived, the room began to look alive. I began filling every niche with my china and porcelain, and the plates that did not fit into the cupboard we hung on the walls.

LEFT I have set my table, a monastery table from Guinivere, for an elegant but relaxed lunch. The dinner plates and finger bowls date from the 19th century, the glasses and napkin rings are handblown by Antony Stern of Battersea, London, and the vases are favorites from my collection. Shops like Habitat and Crate & Barrel offer similar crockery and I have always found flea markets to be good sources.

The room began to take shape, and I searched high and low for a fabric that would be the perfect blue for the room. I finally decided on a Fortuny fabric – and of course, one that had not been produced for simply ages. As there was no stock, we had to have it custom-made and this took some time. Yet when it came, we made so much with it. Along with a silk striped fabric by Bernard Thorpe, we created curtains, shades, a cloth to cover a cheap chipboard round table, and chair seat covers.

By this stage the room was very blue and white, and I decided that I would continue, and make it obsessively blue and white – china for the table, glass, table cloths, pictures for the walls – everything. It became the most successful dining room I had ever had. People loved dining there and, evidently, everyone loved reading – and talking – about it. At the gallery, I still receive many calls enquiring about my blue and white room.

I have now turned my attention to the kitchen (illustrated opposite and on pages 62–63) where a floor-to-ceiling cupboard houses the items in daily use while a hutch contains more precious pieces. It is a very practical room and one that is in constant use. Here I entertain friends informally and I find the conversation so often turns to talk of blue and white. My friend Kate Dyson, whose kitchen hutch is photographed on page 11, also adores blue and white and has a comprehensive collection of blue and white china. My bedroom too, shown on pages 80–81, is hopelessly blue and white, but I can honestly say that I never tire of this combination.

Thus began the germ of an idea about a blue and white book. Not just about blue and white in the conventional sense, but all the shades from indigo through to Swedish blue; I wanted beautiful photographs to showcase fantastic ideas from all over the world. Along with details to show how each look was created, you can see how my favorite colors can act as subtle accents in a room, or study the collections of blue and white arranged to form a wonderfully eclectic style.

This book grew from my endless love affair with blue and white. Although I am almost constantly surrounded and inspired by my favorite colors, it appears that the charm of blue and white is quite inexhaustible.

I owe a big thank you to all those people who allowed me into their blue and white homes, all the fabric houses who let me use their fabrics and, in particular, Isabelle from Pierre Frey; Karen Howes who worked with me on long, hot days to find us what we wanted and never complained; and Julia Lowery at my gallery who found everything each time anyone lost something. And finally a big thank you to Fritz von der Schulenburg whose enthusiasm and taste are infectious. Working with a person who never tires or loses his humor is a delight.

I hope that when looking through this book you will be inspired to find a way to introduce the blue and white look into your own home. We may not live in castles, palaces, or idyllic country retreats, but we can all enjoy the beauty of blue and white living

9

BLUE & WHITE CHINA

RIGHT

The top of the hutch, left to right

1. Deep blue English transfer printed ironstone platter with a fishing scene by Rogers, c. 1820.
2. Blue and white tureen lid, Swansea, chinoiserie pattern, c. 1790.
3. Blue and white teapot, Chinese, late 18th century.
4. English platter, Rogers, a later edition of the first platter on the left, c. 1840.
5. Stone china platter, Staffordshire, 1830s.
6. Chinese willow platter.

The top shelf, left to right

1. Masons ironstone china blue and white jug, c. 1820.
2. Pearlware charger, English, c. 1810.
3. English transfer printed plate, Henry Jetzen, bird pattern, by Thomas Dimmock.
4. Spode Jasmine pattern plate, impressed mark, early 19th century.
5. Early flow blue plate by Wood and Sons, Burslem, a view of Liverpool c. 1810.
6. New Spode repoduction of 1820s botanical pattern plate, one of Spode's most sought-after patterns, dating from the early 1800s.
7. Fairy Villas plate by Maddock and Seddon, Staffordshire, Burslem, 1840s. One of a series of romantic Chinese scenes.
8. Dutch blue and white Delft dish, c. 1770.
9. French blue and white enamel jug, c. 1920.

The center shelf, left to right

1. British scenery by Booths, Tunstall, Staffs, miniature jug, c. 1900.
2. Yuan bird pattern plate by Encoch Wood and Sons. Another popular blue and white pattern, much copied over the years.
3. Booths dessert plate 1876–1883, Indian ornament pattern.
4. 19th-century willow pattern cup, c. 1810, maker unknown. Typical of porcelains made from 1770–1810 when Chinese patterns were fashionable. Willow pattern is the best known one.
5. Minton delft pattern plate, impressed and printed Minton, England, c. 1890–1910.
6. Victorian blue spongeware mug, c. 1850. Sponging is one of the most popular traditional methods of decorating pottery.
7. Village fisherman, pattern plate by J and W Handley and Co, c. 1825.
8. Royal Danish blue and white plate, c. 1920s. This is one of the most famous traditional patterns to be found in the beautiful and much-prized Copenhagen porcelain.
9. Copeland and Garrett transfer printed plate c. 1833, decorated with one of Byron's views – a series of illustrations from a popular book on Byron.
10. "Death of the Bear" by Spode from their famous and rare Indian sporting service, made in 1812.

11. George V flow blue ale mug – a typical pub mug decorated with hops.
12. Rogers farm scene, with ruins in background, cows in foreground.
13. Blue and white floral transfer mug, maker unknown, 1840s.
14. John Stevenson and sons elephant pattern, a later copy of a 1780s transfer.
15. Blue and white spongeware mug 1850.
16. Rogers vine pattern, blue and white, 1784–1836.
17. Blue chinoiserie cup, English porcelain with gilded edge, c. 1810.
18. Miniature gravy boat, willow pattern, c. 1900.

The bottom shelf, left to right

1. Modern Spode blue and white rose mug, a copy of a famous 1825 pattern.
2. Blue and white Greek pattern pearlware plate with arcaded edge.
3. Spode breakfast cup, a new copy of an 1831 transfer.
4. 1880s Minton porcelain plate – oriental-style.
5. (front) Small sheet pattern pearlware saucer, c. 1800. (behind) Continental porcelain plate, late 19th century. The pattern is inspired by a famous Sevres design dating from the 18th century.
6. Early 19th-century chinoiserie saucer with gold edge, c. 1810.
7. Parian ware spotted pitcher – late 19th century – another type of blue and white.
8 & 9. Saucers, early 19th-century chinoiserie with gold bands.
10. Coalport blue and white milk pitcher.
11. Miniature teapot, early 19th-century, Worcester, England.
12. Wedgwood water lily pattern plate, 1822, showing the bold botanical designs, popular at the start of the 19th century.
13. Cornish ware mug.
14. Spode Greek pattern mug, 1806, pattern on new edition.

The front of the hutch, left to right

1. Blue and white pitcher, Caughley M mark.
2. Worcester tea pot and cover.
3. Hot water plate – grazing rabbits, maker unknown, 1820s, one of the most sought-after rare early transfer patterns.
4. Large blue and white pitcher, Chinese, late 18th century.
5. Castleford teapot, c. 1810, with sliding metal lid. Another version of blue and white.
6. Large late 18th-century blue and white Chinese bowl. Chinese influence formed the backbone of European porcelain design.
7. Enamel French butter dish. Yet another version of blue and white, dating from the 1920s.
8. Late 1830s Staffordshire pitcher, blue transfer onto blue body.
9. Miniature blue and white teapot by Meissen – a rare piece dating from the late 18th century and illustrating the best of Continental blue and white.
10. Wedgwood bowl, 1860, applied blue decoration onto creamware body.

ONE

THE WORLD OF
BLUE &
WHITE

LEFT The Sobha Niwas, Hall of Brilliance, situated on the third floor of the Chandra Mahal, which forms part of the City Palace in Jaipur, India and where successive Maharajas entertained.

I HAVE HAD A LIFELONG LOVE AFFAIR WITH BLUE and white in its many variations, but it was not until I started work on this book that I realized the extent to which I shared this obsession with a large proportion of humanity from differing cultures and different times. The world over, there are wonderful examples of buildings, both grand and modest, which have been decorated with this most appealing of color combinations to enrich and brighten the lives of their occupants.

We gain our inspiration from the natural world that surrounds us, in which the range of blues is almost infinite, spanning the whole spectrum from the palest gray-blue to the most intense cerulean. In the natural world the combination of blue and white can be found whenever we look around us, wherever we are – in white-capped seas, white clouds floating in a blue sky, gleaming icicles, vibrant or softly hued blue flowers, shimmering butterflies, iridescent birds – so it is hardly surprising that these colors have always inspired us.

LEFT Sunlight filters through hundreds of small holes in the domed roof of this Turkish bath in Bursa, where it reflects on the surface of the turquoise water in the pool, throwing light into the recesses.

ABOVE Graded dark blue tiles follow the contour of these swimming pool steps. The main area of the pool is laid with turquoise tiles and the rim edged with a simple pattern.

RIGHT The interior of a mosque in the Turkish town of Konja. The walls have been tiled in a turquoise frieze, leading the eye up into the dome. The dome is tiled with a range of intricate motifs.

We have always decorated our homes, our domestic wares, and our clothing, often as a way of recording the natural life we see around us. This instinct to embellish is the mark of a culture moving away from survival toward civilization, which is why the cultural heritage of the great civilizations is so rich. The skill of the craftsmen of Byzantium, Ancient Greece and Rome, and the Renaissance is as much a marvel today as it was then.

In earliest times the primary source of color came, quite simply, from the earth; tribes in Britain daubed their bodies with blue clay as a form of decoration. The clay was colored with woad, a blue plant dye. Another source of blue was the anil plant which gave us indigo, a deep blue pigment used to color cloth. Indigo is still an important pigment and it is used by everyone from local craftsmen in the developing world to the leading fashion houses of Europe.

The Middle East was the cradle that nurtured blue, and it was the discovery of the cobalt blue pigment, probably in Baluchistan, which introduced this wonderful intense blue into the decorative arts of both that region and the many parts of the world with which it traded. Byzantine and Islamic mosaics and Chinese porcelain would all have been poor shadows of their glorious hues had the craftsmen been without this color; and it was the drive to emulate these beautiful and much-coveted wares which led to the development of the European porcelain industry.

Today it is hard to imagine a world where paint was a luxury and color was very restricted, yet in the past artists who wished to use vibrant colors had to make their own paints, grinding pigments and blending them to achieve the desired color and texture. Craftsmen would wait anxious months for precious minerals perilously transported by camel train and by sea, then would risk their own lives by blending the toxic substances to create the color they desired.

Given the danger associated with this color, its social impact was tremendous. The jewel-like painted interiors of the great churches and palaces with their frescoes and magnificent paintings were a startling contrast to the simpler homes of the general populace, helping to confirm the power and glory of the ecclesiastical and aristocratic elite.

Then with the advent of wooden houses it became necessary to protect the wood from the destructive elements. Initially this was done with tar or bitumen, but these materials were slowly replaced with oil-based paints, the forerunners of the modern paints we use today.

RIGHT The magnificent ballroom in the former British Embassy in Istanbul is dominated by two huge crystal chandeliers. Elegant white columns add a classical focus and divide the pale blue walls at regular intervals, with detailing around the mirrors and ceiling picked out in gilt.

LEFT The magnificent white pagodas of a Buddhist temple stand out against the dark blue of a Burmese sky. Some are ornately carved and others tapered. The points of each pagoda are adorned with intricate gilt helmets.

RIGHT This detail of the spire of a Turkish mosque in Konja shows extraordinary workmanship. The roof and walls have been covered with turquoise tiles, the contours of the scalloped design adding texture to its beautiful shape.

OPPOSITE A Chinese-style pavilion stands in a Swedish park. Its simple wooden door is made infinitely more elegant by the positioning of two columns on either side of it. A scallop motif outlined in dark blue has been painted above the door.

Islamic art is justifiably famed for the superlative quality of its mosaics, ceramics, enameling, and glass. Islamic ruling forbids all representational art and has concentrated instead on the development of a fantastic repertoire of intricate decorative patterns based on geometric forms and calligraphy. The use of precious or luxurious materials is also condemned and it is these prohibitions that, far from stultifying creativity, have brought about the magnificent flowering of Islamic art which can be seen in its great buildings, its gardens, its pottery, and its carpets.

Glazed bricks, tiles, and mosaics were routinely used to apply a decorative and durable finish to buildings. Blue, turquoise, and green were the colors most frequently used. Each color was fired separately to insure that it was as intense as possible and the stunning results are still as brilliant today as when they were made. Mosaics were made in many elaborate shapes which would fit together to make panels of startling intricacy.

The finest examples of Islamic decorative art are to be found in their pottery. The establishment of trade routes to China meant that the two cultures inspired one another. Some of the earliest developments in Islamic pottery can be traced to fragments of imported Chinese pottery; and conversely tin glazed pottery with blue decoration by the Abassid potters is believed to have inspired the earliest Chinese blue and white porcelain.

19

ABOVE A classical bust on a marble pedestal graces an Irish ballroom.

ABOVE LEFT A detail of the painted overdoor in the dining room at Hylinge in Sweden shows two lions appropriately feasting on a bowl of fruit.

BELOW LEFT Two griffins form the focal point of this detail of a Swedish tiled stove. The tiles are painted with a neo-classical design.

RIGHT The edge of an exquisite Russian table which has been decorated with onyx, marble, and other semi-precious stones and also ornamented with gilt. The top is made from lapis lazuli.

The Moorish invasion brought many elements of Islamic art into European culture, particularly the use of highly glazed tiles and mosaics. In Spain and Portugal the long tradition of manufacturing high-quality blue and white tiles continues to this day and they can be seen as decorative features on many fine buildings, from the restrained beauty of the Alhambra to the colorful exuberance of Gaudí. As the Moorish influence spread it could be traced throughout Europe in pottery and ceramics – the faience of France, Dutch Delft, and Italian Maiolica all showed Moorish as well as Chinese influence. The calligraphic designs based on Arabic script became purely decorative devices with no understanding of what they had originally represented.

ABOVE Details from a selection of tiles:
An Iznik tile from Turkey with a beautiful and traditional design (above left). Fragments of Ottoman tiles (below left). Inlaid tiles from a building in Konja (above right).

RIGHT An Iznik tile panel from the wall of the Arab Hall which is the centerpiece of Leighton House in London. The Arab Hall was created as a setting for the tiles Leighton had acquired on his travels in the East. It was designed by George Aitchison and based on the banqueting room at La Zisa, a Moorish palace in Palermo.

22

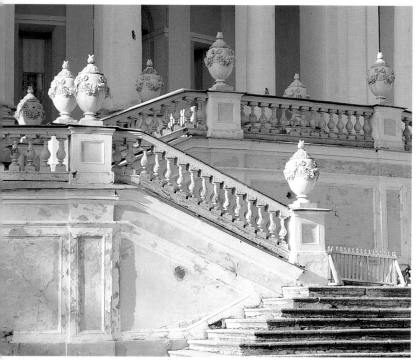

ABOVE A Federal-style, 18th-century clapboard exterior of a timber-framed church at the center of a New England village.

LEFT An ornate balustrade of the 18th-century rococo Montagnes Russes pavilion on the Oranienbaum estate outside St Petersburg.

RIGHT A new look at Colonial style with this Walt Disney interpretation, adopted for a hotel at Disney World in Florida.

The practice of covering the exteriors of our houses with paint is a recent development. Its primary purpose is to protect the building, but the decorative element has always been a consideration. You need only look at houses painted in colors from Wedgwood blue to oxblood red to realize that paint is more than a protective coating. When it comes to external decoration we should be guided by the colors around us – those that work best will be a reflection of the landscape. Hot intense colors look wonderful in Mexico, but gaudy and inappropriate in New England, whereas subtle colors are lost among the riotous palette of Latin America.

LEFT Rooftop sculpture by the Spanish architect, Antoni Gaudí, graced a selection of the houses he designed in Barcelona. Often of bizarre shape and randomly decorated with bits of tile, these sculptures also had a practical function, serving as chimneys and ventilation ducts.

RIGHT This detail illustrates the random mixing of broken pieces of tile and ceramic that was to become identified as Gaudí's trademark.

BELOW RIGHT Fragments of Portuguese and Chinese porcelain have been patiently fashioned into the shape of an ornamental duck.

In man-made as well as natural settings, the many shades and tones of blue blend easily and harmoniously. Modern skyscrapers clad in reflective glass become mirror images of the sky and clouds around them. The white surfaces of the Sydney Opera House are thrown into dramatic relief against the blue of the sky and the waters of Sydney harbor. In seaside towns and villages around the world blue and white is the most frequently used color combination, from the Greek islands to Cape Cod; shades of blue stand in sharp contrast to pure white. Even in the most unnatural and built-up of surroundings it is difficult to associate ugliness with blue. Rarely does a shade of blue, even at its most vibrant, strike a discordant note.

27

PREVIOUS PAGES Architecture around the world has used color to outline entrances, exaggerate doorways, and embellish walls. Nationally idiosyncratic, these examples illustrate the attractive wooden shutters of a stable block in Austria; an imposing doorway in Minorca, surrounded by inlaid fragments of tile; the use of dark blue paint, both flat and gloss finishes, to enhance a white wall in Mexico and even a simple outline in blue around a door frame.

LEFT The bright colors of purple and turquoise from opposite ends of the blue spectrum are embellished by the ornate wooden trellis and porch of this gingerbread house on the island of Mustique in the Caribbean.

RIGHT A restricted view of a narrow street through the window of a house in Goa. The clear panes, alternating with those of purple and turquoise, filter the harsh sunlight and throw interesting flashes of cooling color around the interior of the room.

FAR RIGHT The exterior of a simple Welsh farmhouse gleams under a fresh coat of whitewash, the woodwork and cornerstones painted a contrasting bright blue.

As we look through the pages of this chapter with all the magnificent examples of the world of blue and white, and read the romantic stories of their making, it can be a dilemma to know how to apply what we have seen to our own lives. Few of us have a castle, a painted palace, or even a picturesque ruin, and while we can admire, we also need help to know how we can use these ideas effectively in our own homes.

It can, in fact, be very simple indeed – it may be a particular blue which is just the shade we wish to use on a wall, for kitchen tiles, or to paint a piece of furniture. Paint suppliers can now mix any color paint you might want in gloss, satin, or flat finishes and you should not hesitate to ask for their help. Take along the picture that has inspired you; very few people can accurately hold a color in their head. With computer-controlled paint mixing, suppliers can now accurately match a color from a swatch of fabric, a piece of china, or a picture, but if you are having a color custom-mixed, be sure to get enough to finish your job to avoid unsightly variations in a second batch of paint.

This book can also inspire you to be more bold in your use of color. When planning a blue and white color scheme, you may picture a fairly conventional blue and white palette, but on turning these pages it will quickly become apparent that blue encompasses a vast range of hues, from deep purple to soft aqua, and that mixing blues together is an exciting option.

A mosaic pattern can be the inspiration for a stenciled border. Traced off the page it can be photocopied, and if necessary enlarged, and then used to cut a simple stencil. A painted room in a palace can be scaled down and the elements of its design incorporated in a room of more modest proportions. A picture of a doorway with a broad band of color painted around it reveals that this can create the illusion of a much larger entrance – a cheap and easy to achieve transformation.

Each picture should be viewed as a starting point from which you can develop your own ideas. To create your own world of blue and white you need to be inspired and it is far better to be inspired by the best than by the mediocre.

31

TWO

LIVING IN BLUE & WHITE

LEFT Imposing classical busts on gilded pedestals line a wall of this Irish ballroom, alternately interspersed with gilt-framed mirrors and intricately painted panels. The classical theme is continued with a line of busts on marble columns.

DECORATING WITH BLUE AND WHITE HAS always been a magical formula. From earliest history to the present day, this combination of colors seems to have blended easily with the fashions and fancies of the period. What is the secret of its continuing success? First and foremost, it is a fail-safe formula: it is almost impossible to make mistakes as all shades of blue seem to complement one another. Secondly, despite being one of the most tried and tested combinations in the history of interior design, it retains a marvelous freshness. It never seems drab or passé, and always appeals. And finally, it remains, to my mind, one of the easiest and most restful decorative schemes to live with.

In this chapter we show examples of living rooms that illustrate the versatility of blue and white. A glance at the pictures will show just how varied any interpretation can be. From the grandest of rooms to the most simple, these colors are guaranteed to combine harmoniously and give each room an inviting air of serenity and tranquility.

33

LEFT A quiet corner off the master bedroom in this Majorcan farmhouse, designed by Mimmi O'Connell, uses bold blue and white stripes and patterned cotton rugs to create a cool contrast against the overall whiteness.

RIGHT Underfurnished simplicity in this small room near the Bosphorus river in Turkey. The louvered shutters filter the sunlight that reflects off the water outside, creating a soft, hazy interior.

It is sometimes stated that blue is a cold color, to which I would say that blue can certainly be cool, but need never be cold. The geographical spectrum of blues is ample proof of this – from the sparkling white and palest ice-blue of snowy landscapes in the extreme north, to the intense blues of the Mediterranean, shades of blue deepen and become warmer with the climate.

At its simplest, blue and white living is to be seen in the houses of the Greek islands where roughcast walls are colorwashed in chalky blues or whites, with woodwork and furniture painted in contrasting shades of blue or brilliant white; or in the bleached-out colors of the whitewashed cottages that border the coasts of northern Europe.

ABOVE The narrow entrance hall to architect Paula Navone's Milan flat. The industrial metal staircase leads up to the living room in this loft conversion. The blue-tiled floor and washed, faded denim walls are linked at floor level with a neat row of blue and white tiles.

RIGHT Simplicity in these surroundings creates an attractive, tranquil atmosphere in this peaceful homestead. The plaster and wood have been whitewashed and the wooden table beneath the small window is covered with a simple white cloth. An old cotton quilt hangs over the balustrade.

LEFT There can never be too much of a good thing! Here designers Private Lives have confidently combined fabrics, ceramic vases and ornaments, books, and even flowers to create an overall blue and white effect.

To my mind, our whole approach to color has changed over the last decade or two and we are now open to a much stronger palette. With the advent of specialist paint ranges it is no longer simply a matter of choosing a paint color, we also choose the finish we want – there are colorwashes, limewashes, scumble glazes, and varnishes applied with stippling brushes, graining combs, sponges, and the many other tools that were once solely the province of the specialist decorator, but are now familiar to most of us. Television programs on home decoration were once only to be seen during the day, but are now mainstream evening entertainment with the experts becoming media stars. Stenciled borders and friezes are everyday decorative techniques which most of us have tried, and as we have become more experimental we have learned how to balance the proportions of our rooms with pattern and color. Manufacturers are producing ranges of historic colors using natural pigments to produce opaque shades of great depth and subtlety which look just as wonderful in a modern home as they do in a period setting, and despite their premium price we are prepared to pay the extra to achieve the effect we desire.

As we become more confident with color, so we are more adventurous with pattern and will mix together checks, stripes, and florals drawn from the incredible variety of fabrics on the market. Given the ease with which blues of every hue can be used alongside one another, you can introduce a surprising number of patterns without its looking messy, especially if you use some plain blue or white fabric to pull it all together.

When it comes to blue and white decorative objects to use as finishing touches, we are spoiled for choice – whatever our taste or scale of investment. You may well find it is more a case of knowing when to stop than how to start.

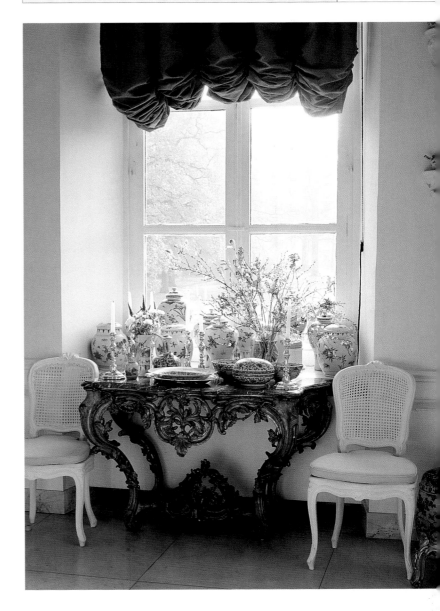

ABOVE A collection of blue and white ginger jars, vases, bowls, and plates adorn a giltwood side-table beneath one window of this classical dining room.

39

RIGHT These stunning vases are part of Axel Vervoordt's collection of 17th-century Ming porcelain from The Hatcher Collection, salvaged by Captain Hatcher from the South China Sea. Purchasers of these pieces included the British Museum, Berlin's Charlottenberg Palace and the Boston Museum of Fine Arts, but Axel Vervoordt's collection graces his dining room, where the table's mirrored surface reflects their beauty across the room.

LEFT, ABOVE AND RIGHT The dining room at the Castle of s-Gravenwezel, the home of interior decorator and antiques dealer, Axel Vervoordt, is decorated in shades of white and palest blue reminiscent of the Swedish palette. The colors provide a setting for his magnificent collection of blue and white Ming porcelain. Although the glaze has degraded slightly after its long submergence, the romance of the shipwreck and the fact that the collection included designs never seen before meant that its value has remained high.

Of course the inspiration for your room need not come from a color chart; the starting point may be a beautiful length of fabric, a painting, or a collection of porcelain. A precious object can be the focal point from which the rest of the room develops. With blue and white decorating you can choose an almost monochromatic palette such as that used in the room featured on these pages, where a white color scheme is the perfect foil for a prized collection of Chinese blue and white porcelain. It is interesting to picture how different the effect would have been had the owner chosen to set the collection against blue walls rather than white.

ABOVE The clean lines of this white biscuit medallion provide a striking contrast in color and pattern to the blue and white toile fabric behind.

LEFT The dressing room to the bedroom which once belonged to Baroness Ottiliana Liljencrantz at Sturehof in Sweden. Simply furnished, as the neo-classical style dictated, the room has walls with mouldings painted by Lars Bolander, who is renowned for his mural decoration.

RIGHT This semicircular Empire bench, with elaborate armrests at either end designed in the shape of a lion's foot, is located in the Schinckel Pavilion in the park at Charlottenburg Castle, Berlin. The pavilion was designed by Karl-Friedrich Schinckel in 1824.

RIGHT The cool living room of a summer house overlooking Bodrum harbor in Turkey. Designed for comfort and relaxation, the cool marble floor is softened with huge scatter pillows and long, low banquettes, all in creamy white.

Unless you are a supremely confident decorator it is helpful when planning a blue and white room to follow the example of the professionals and prepare a color board. This involves gathering a selection of swatches of fabric in your chosen colors and mounting them on a piece of cardboard painted with the colors to be used on the walls and woodwork. Propped up and viewed from a distance this will give you a preview of the effect you will be creating and allow you to correct any potentially time-wasting and costly mistakes. When you have finalized your choice of colors and fabrics, make a note of them on the color board and keep this as a record for future redecorating.

The effect of daylight on color is an important consideration when decorating a room. A white wall in direct light can be dazzling, but will look quite gray in shadow. Before painting a room you can check the effect of direct and reflected light on the various surfaces by painting plain, inexpensive paper with your chosen color and attaching it to the walls. This is particularly important at the corners of the room where reflection can dramatically alter colors. The type of paint you use will also have an effect on the interplay of light and color. Flat paint absorbs light while silk, satin, or gloss paint will reflect light with the result that the same color can look very different, depending on the finish used. Flat paint is better at disguising irregularities on wall surfaces because of its non-reflective properties, while satin or gloss paint will add life to dark rooms.

Artificial light is, by its very nature, much more controllable than natural light, but it too will have an effect on the colors in your room. Halogen bulbs are recommended for pure, natural light. You may find this rather cold-looking when used with pale colors, in which case tinted incandescent bulbs will give a warmer light.

LEFT This elegant double staircase was designed by David Hicks for a neo-Palladian villa in Portugal. The flat wood balusters stand out against the air-force blue of the walls and the smart gray stair carpet.

ABOVE A painting by Elsworth Kelly and a sculpture of two chairs by Dakota Jackson occupy pride of place in a modern loft conversion in New York.

Using deep shades on the walls of your living room is a very positive statement which initially requires some courage, but can be much more interesting to look at and live in than "safer" pale shades. If you feel apprehensive you can experiment on a small scale with an entry or hall that adjoins a larger room. Once you have gained confidence you will find that dark walls are a marvelous backdrop for any collection of paintings or porcelain, which is thrown into sharp relief, especially when the wall color echoes or pleasingly contrasts with a color used on the decorative objects. I love to decorate in this positive way as I feel that it conveys my approach to life and helps me create a home that is both relaxing and stimulating.

49

ABOVE The look of a room can be changed instantly by putting chairs into slipcovers. This corner of a country living room is dominated by the scent of a mass of garden roses on a carved three-legged African table.

RIGHT This large living room designed by John Stefanidis has comfortable chairs and sofas which in summer are covered in blue and white ticking, fresh-looking stripes, and ikats. The room is always full of flowers from the garden, bowls of roses, and plants from the greenhouse.

Decorating in blue and white can be anything from a complete all-over effect with walls, curtains, upholstery, and accessories all conforming to the same theme, to an almost monochrome approach with just touches of blue or, turning that idea on its head, shades of blue-on-blue highlighted with accents of white. Although these are undoubtedly the dominant colors for the blue and white room, you should not be afraid of introducing other colors. It's amazing how a splash of contrasting color can add drama; imagine just one orange silk pillow in an otherwise Mediterranean blue and white room, or a single shocking pink rose among a collection of blue and white china. The color theme is emphasized by deliberate deviation and becomes more exciting.

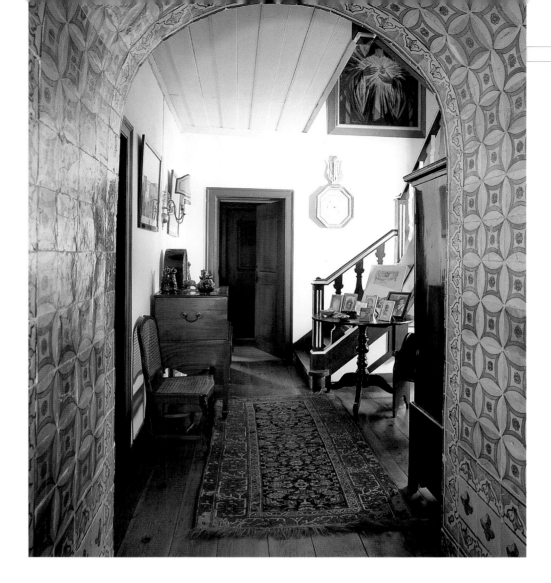

LEFT The stairs, entrance hall, and even the windowsill and surround of this 18th-century villa in Cascais are lined with blue and white Portuguese tiles. The walls of the staircase are asymmetrical — one is tiled with a complete image, while the opposite wall carries a frieze to window height.

RIGHT A simpler, less sophisticated pattern of tiles has been used to line this doorway leading into the hall of a Portuguese country house.

Like the other colors of the spectrum, the color blue has many associations with the natural and artistic worlds. Yet we also respond to blue in a personal sense, and it is for this reason that we often have an emotional reaction, however subtle, to the use of blue in decoration and design. We feel colors as well as see them. A visit to Provence may well inspire me to decorate a sunny room in the hazy summer colors of that place with the cerulean blue of the sky, the deep purply-blue of lavender and gray-green of the foliage. My enjoyment of that room will not be restricted to an appreciation of a successful color scheme, it will also recall the warmth of the Provençal sun and the scents and tastes of the south of France.

Mysteriously, you may find yourself moved to tears by the intense blue used by Chagall in his paintings, or the blue of a Madonna's robes, and feel drawn to search for paintings or decorative objects that echo the color; or repeatedly find yourself using a particular soft shade of blue which would not usually be to your taste, only to discover that it was the exact color of a favorite childhood room.

Blue is a calm, sometimes even passive color and has an air of tranquility about it. It is a color you can sink into and under its influence lose yourself in rêverie. Much used in Christian art, it is the color of faith; to the Chinese, with its long tradition of blue and white porcelain, the color signifies immortality.

LEFT A living room in a villa on the island of Mustique in the Caribbean is furnished with a combination of bamboo-style and traditional sofas and day beds for comfort and coolness. The limed roof is raised to take advantage of the on-shore breeze.

RIGHT The late 18th-century salon at Bernshammar in Sweden has elaborate painted wall decorations by Pehr Emanuel Limnell. Between the windows are two mirrors with matching side tables by Pehr Ljung. The plain wooden floor has been stenciled to resemble more expensive parquet.

If you are starting from scratch with a room, choosing the colors to use can be a daunting process; it is often much easier if you have something around from which to make your selection whether it is a page torn from a magazine, a prized piece of blue and white china, or a wonderful piece of fabric you have seen. Either way you will want to choose shades that enhance the feeling you wish to create in the room. For this reason it is helpful to remember that cool blues are those with yellow in them, in other words the turquoises, blue greens, and aquamarines, while the warm blues have red in them and include the rich royal blues, purples, and lavenders. Gray is a useful neutral color which can be used alongside blue and white without diluting either color. Like blue, gray comes in warm and cool tones, and the choice of gray should be made from the same end of the spectrum as the blues you have chosen.

The sense of crisp freshness that a blue and white scheme conveys can be used to advantage in any type of living space – from an informal family room or a book-lined study to the grandest of formal living rooms. A sitting room furnished with comfortable sofas covered in flowered blue and white chintz, alongside antique pine furniture, with walls painted periwinkle blue and hung with striped draperies in harmonizing shades would make a welcome gathering place for all the family and will withstand misuse surprisingly well, while a contemporary study painted in cool blues and furnished with simple clean-lined bookshelves and a stylish desk will create a calm haven for creative thought. A large formal living room has the scale and proportions eminently suited to the subtle palette of Scandinavian colors. These colors will heighten the elegance of their surroundings and age with grace and dignity, as befits a room of this style.

55

THREE

DINING IN BLUE & WHITE

LEFT The neo-classical dining room at Hylinge, Sweden, is decorated in blue and gray. The coupled Corinthian pilasters are painted onto the wall. The dining chairs are modern copies of a Hepplewhite design adapted from a Gustavian set also at Hylinge.

THE AREAS IN THE HOME WHERE FOOD IS prepared and eaten offer a myriad of settings for some of the most beautiful and natural effects in blue and white, be it a formal dining room, relaxed kitchen, sunroom, or shaded porch. There is an interpretation of blue and white which will enhance each room and appeal to you whether your taste is for clean simplicity or lavish opulence. And because blue and white "layers" so successfully it can be used freely on walls, furnishings, and accessories.

THE BLUE & WHITE DINING ROOM

In the dining room a blue and white scheme has the advantage of looking fresh and light during the day and vibrantly rich and decorative at night. No other color scheme can successfully achieve such a dramatic change of mood, and the many shades of blue and white offer an extraordinarily versatile range of colors from the palest of hues where white and blue are almost indistinguishable, to the startling contrasts of dazzling white and ultramarine.

57

LEFT AND RIGHT An elegant conservatory-dining room in the home of the interior designer Nina Campbell. The table is set for an informal lunch using blue and white china and glass which blend superbly with Nina's fabrics. Blue and purple "witches' balls" look wonderful in a wire basket hung from the ceiling. A close-up of the table (left) shows the variety of blues that have been used – a dark blue underplate with a blue on white white dinner plate topped by a white on blue soup bowl, accompanied by three different colors of glass.

The pale light and landscape of Scandinavia are characterized by cool gray-blues and were the inspiration for the restrained and elegant decoration of the Gustavian palaces of Sweden; but you need live neither in a palace nor in Scandinavia to make use of this understated palette of colors. To achieve a similarly subtle quality of light in warmer, brighter latitudes the light may be filtered through muslin curtains or shutters. A collection of Royal Danish blue and white porcelain would look perfectly at home in a room decorated in these gentle hues.

In the classic English tradition, a gleaming mahogany table looks marvelous laid with blue and white china and topped with crisp white damask napkins. There is a long history of fine dinnerware in this color combination including the Staffordshire potteries of Spode, Minton, and Wedgwood, and should you be fortunate enough to own such a dinner service it will be displayed to perfection on such a table. Equally there is great charm in a harlequin table setting of blue and white china from many different sources, and the overall effect is so entrancing that the individual pieces can be of quite modest provenance.

In hot climates, the intense electric blues and dazzling whites of the Mediterranean and Caribbean are as appropriate used indoors as outdoors. The shady interior of a dining room that uses these colors both looks and feels cooler and provides a welcome retreat from the sun – a place where diners are happy to linger long after the meal is over. Louvered shutters or rattan shades at the windows will keep light levels low but still allow good air circulation. Traditional Spanish or Portuguese blue and white tiles fit well into these surroundings and a table setting of Provençal pottery with its robust textures and designs accompanied by brilliant blue hand-blown glasses, such as those from Biot in the south of France, will provide the finishing touches to a simple but sophisticated room.

TOP LEFT The alcoves in this kitchen are "splashed" with blue and white in the style of the porcelain made by the Gemundener Keramik factory. The shelves are filled with pots from Morocco, Japan, and Persia, mixed with 19th-century Staffordshire. A blue and white tablecloth, napkins, tumblers, and candles complete the effect.

BELOW LEFT The kitchen has been given the same tile treatment throughout, the table laid on this occasion with a crisp checked tablecloth and Gemundener Keramik plates and bowls.

RIGHT A plain, scrubbed square table is laid for a simple lunch. The chairs are designed by John Stefanidis and the gouache above the sideboard is by Teddy Millington-Drake.

BELOW A blue glass vase filled with fresh flowers stands on the kitchen windowsill.

There is something about the random display of blue and white plates and dishes, tureens and platters, earthenware and fine porcelain, that delights the eye and warms the heart, and I consider no blue and white dining room complete without some of these decorative pieces, grouped together on a side table, arranged on an antique hutch, or even mounted on a wall.

At night, add drama to your blue and white dining room by spreading a sumptuous blue velvet cloth on the table and set it with an array of blue candles in silver candlesticks, sparkling water in blue glass bottles, an arrangement of flowers in a blue and gold toleware container, and vibrant blue glassware. By standing the flower arrangement on a mirror you can multiply the impact of the blooms and reflect the sparkle of the candlelight around the table. All these details and more can easily be added to create a richly opulent effect for your dinner party.

61

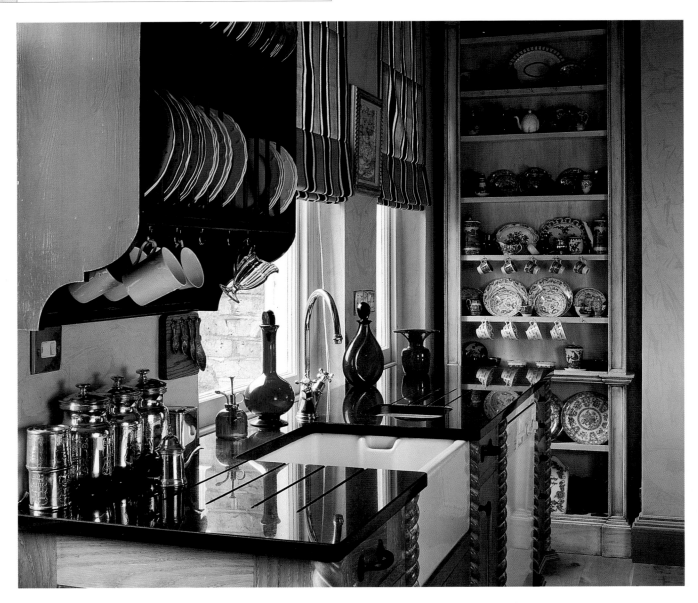

ABOVE AND RIGHT My kitchen is a furnished rather than a built-in kitchen and is an immensely practical room, but also wonderfully decorative as it houses my lifetime's collection of blue and white china, glass, and paintings. A floor-to-ceiling china cupboard houses the blue and white items in daily use and the pine plate rack displays my collection of china. The blue central unit, which I designed and had built by Simon Saunders, houses my kitchen utensils.

LEFT Kate Dyson's collection of blue and white china is stored in similar style on a plate rack.

62

LEFT Blue floor tiles characterize architect Paula Navone's home. The kitchen is no exception, where she has used turquoise glazed tiles as a backsplash behind an almost industrial stainless steel oven.

RIGHT A cast-iron range is a fashion prerequisite for all country houses and is available in many colors, including blue.

BELOW RIGHT No detail has been overlooked here as even the pitcher, saucepans, and curtain match the color scheme.

THE BLUE & WHITE KITCHEN

The use of blue and white in the kitchen has a long tradition. Most countries have traditional designs of tiles and pottery that use these colors and they remain enduringly popular because of the calm, fresh quality they bring. I was moving house as I was working on this book and had planned a scheme for my new kitchen that was not remotely connected to blue and white, but as we prepared these pages and took the photographs to illustrate them, I was lured away from my original ideas as I reached the conclusion that blue and white was the freshest and prettiest combination and that nothing I could think of would surpass it. All my other schemes were put aside and once I had found one or two pieces of furniture painted in that marvelous French slate-blue, the rest simply followed on. By combining painted furniture with other pieces in plain oak, an un-built-in look was achieved, and I completed the effect with striped fabric shades and masses of blue and white china.

Blue and white for the kitchen need not be expensive. A hutch laden with blue and white china doesn't have to be filled with priceless treasures to delight the eye. Odd plates and cups look enchanting displayed together and a chipped pitcher can have a new lease on life filled with garden flowers. Old French enamelware uses the blue and white theme on everything from pitchers to soup ladles. It looks charming in the kitchen and can still be collected inexpensively.

65

LEFT In this blue kitchen, the maple wood table, chairs and Corian work surfaces are a welcome relief from the solid use of one color.

RIGHT The backsplash around the walls is made up of predominantly white tiles, interspersed at regular intervals with blue ones, on which a further pattern of paler blue has been applied.

Blue and white is so wonderfully versatile that it lends itself to every sort of kitchen. You can opt for all-modern or all-traditional or create an innovative combination of the two using, for instance, a beautiful old blue and white nineteenth-century bowl as a centerpiece alongside contemporary, dishwasher-friendly china, glass, and cutlery. Clean-cut, all-white units create a monochrome setting for bold blue china and cookware, while a pretty blue and white tablecloth transforms the kitchen table into something smarter for evening suppers.

Essentials, too, can play on the blue and white theme with dish towels, trash cans, dishpans, utensils, and canisters all easily and cheaply available.

67

RIGHT A close-up of my kitchen table laid for lunch with my favorite handblown blue glass napkin rings by Anthony Stern of Battersea, London.

In a traditional kitchen the windows can be hung with crisp blue and white curtains in checked gingham or striped dishcloth fabric and with the addition of a cozy blue cast-iron range you will have achieved the essence of the country kitchen. You can almost smell the baking bread and touch the scrubbed surface of the old pine table.

The innate beauty of blue and white china, pottery, and porcelain lends itself to display rather than concealment. Why hide these beautiful objects away in cabinets when they can make their own contribution to the decoration of the kitchen? A pretty plate rack above the sink is both practical and decorative, while open shelves and tiled alcoves allow you to view a selection of many of your favorite blue and white treasures. A traditional hutch is still one of the prettiest ways of displaying china and, even if space is a problem, a shallow hutch can be placed against a wall that would not be deep enough for conventional kitchen cabinets. Blue and white comes in so many different shades, all of which can, and do, mix successfully together, so limiting yourself to a particular style, color, or design is purely a matter of personal preference. Deep blue glass looks wonderful displayed among blue and white china as it intensifies the blue in the patterns, while clear glass seems to take on an extra sparkle in this setting.

ALFRESCO BLUE & WHITE DINING

No matter what the climate, all of us enjoy eating alfresco at some time during the year, and once again, the blue and white theme is perfect for outdoor living. A wicker picnic hamper filled with rustic blue and white china, unpacked onto a hand-woven cloth spread with delicious summer fruits, salads, and crusty bread will look temptingly inviting.

ABOVE Undecorated white porcelain figurines are a pleasing contrast to the many different shades of blue in this pretty table setting.

RIGHT A dining room by Genevieve Weaver uses blue and white china and glass to create color accents on the walls, on top of the elaborate gilt console table, and in the table settings. The warm tones of this room reflect in the superb Venetian glass mirror to create the perfect ambience for evening entertaining.

ABOVE LEFT A table set with blue and white china and clear glasses is perfect for open-air dining in the welcoming shade of a covered terrace in a garden on the island of Mustique.

ABOVE RIGHT Irises and Queen Anne's lace replace the sunflowers, a blue and white tablecloth designed by Lillian Williams is draped over the rustic table and the scene is set for a more formal lunch on this cool terrace.

RIGHT Scattered pillows provide all the comfort neeeded for an impromptu breakfast in the shadow of an old fig tree. This garden in Majorca was originally designed by Cecil Beaton.

LEFT Gigantic "sprinkle-effect" plates from the Gemundener Keramik factory in Austria, dark blue glasses and paler blue linen napkins, flatware with dark blue handles and a riot of sunflowers from the neighboring field will combine well for an alfresco lunch.

71

Under a shady tree in the backyard, a table covered with a blue cloth is a cool haven from the summer sun. Use a blue tablecloth even when the table is not in direct sunlight as it is more restful on the eye in bright light than white. A pitcher of white daisies is a charmingly informal decoration which will go equally well with plain white china or a blue and white pattern. A summer picnic looks particularly inviting when spread on a checked blue and white cloth.

Even in the most agreeable climate, it is not always possible to eat outdoors, and here porches and pavilions come into their own, providing many of the benefits of outdoor eating without the discomforts. With table and chairs permanently in place, the table can be spread at a moment's notice with a cotton cloth and blue and white china, to offer a perfect setting for breakfast in the gentle morning sunshine, an informal lunch with friends, or a romantic candlelit dinner. A posy of fresh flowers from the garden will complete the picture.

LEFT Simple metal shelving has been installed in two alcoves in this Italian kitchen. Lined with highly glazed turquoise tiles, the alcoves house a motley collection of pitchers and glassware. The whitewashed wall is decorated with an unusual tile design where it meets the tiled floor.

ABOVE A collection of creamware is stored on a shelf along a wall lined with an assortment of modern blue and white tiles.

RIGHT A four-drawer flatware box, silver table ornaments, glass, and porcelain are stored away in this neatly kept pantry.

ABOVE AND LEFT A detail of the plate rack in my kitchen, showing a favorite set of French chocolate pots and some of my collection of 19th-century Bristol Blue glass. The swans are among my favorite blue and white pieces. I believe that they were made in Portugal in the 19th century from fragments of 17th- and 18th-century Chinese ceramics.

RIGHT A single white shelf cuts across the uniformity of a wall of assorted blue and white tiles. where items in daily use, such as a stack of glasses and a coffee set of local pottery, are kept for easy access.

THE SUNROOM DINING ROOM

Sunrooms make wonderful dining rooms, since these days, few of them are devoted simply to plants; instead they are rooms that have all the light and airiness of the outdoors, but thanks to modern technology, remain warm and comfortable even in mid-winter. Decorated in blue and white, a sunroom will always look fresh and welcoming. Some colors look fussy and drab against a backdrop of greenery, but blue and white retains its charm. Metalwork benches and chairs painted in the traditional Georgian blue-gray look marvelous in a sunroom when they are piled high with plump cushions upholstered in blue and white ticking, bold stripes and checks. Fabric or rattan shades or blinds hung at the windows and in the roof are essential for shade or to shut out bad weather. For a summer lunch a table setting of blue and white china always looks stunning with vases of bright blue cornflowers, while the spring table with miniature pots of grape hyacinths and lily of the valley is a perfect synthesis of food and flowers.

At night a sunroom makes the most romantic of dining rooms. Lit by candlelight, a table setting of delicate blue and white china, rich blue glass, and antique silver will sparkle and reflect in the glass which surrounds it, and when further embellished with arrangements of fragrant white lilies and roses will provide the perfect setting for the perfect meal.

75

FOUR

SLEEPING IN BLUE & WHITE

LEFT This imposing bedroom is dominated by a superb 19th-century Anglo-Indian four-poster bed. The walls are covered with Indian cotton dhurries. On the bed is finely cut French linen topped with a periwinkle-blue handmade quilt.

NOWHERE DOES THE COMBINATION OF BLUE and white seem more appropriate than in the bedroom. It is restful, tranquil, cool, calming, unfussy, decorative – the list of adjectives seems endless – and as the illustrations for this chapter show, although the palette is limited, the interpretations of it are not.

Once again I feel that the reasons lie with nature, with the ever-present combinations of sky and cloud, sea and sky, light and shade. Blue and white is a natural union, and a union with which we, quite naturally, feel comfortable and at peace.

The bedroom is a very personal room to decorate. It is not just a room to sleep in but also a private retreat from the world outside, somewhere to recharge batteries and take time off from the pressures of life. In my bedroom I dress, do my hair and makeup, and surround myself with personal, pretty things. It is a place where I feel free to indulge myself. In creating an atmosphere which is conducive to all these things it is hardly surprising that blue and white often features in some way or another.

ABOVE This small bedroom is located in one of the guest wings at Elgahammar, considered to be Sweden's finest Palladian house and designed by the architect Giacomo Quarenghi from St Petersburg. The deceptively simple iron-framed bed is clad in a thin-striped blue and white fabric, its spartan appearance softened by the contrasting bed hanging. The chairs and chest of drawers are Biedermeier.

LEFT The twin brass beds and matching wallpaper and furnishing fabric give this bedroom in the same house a more modern feel. The Biedermeier sofa at the end of the two beds provides the only historical footnote.

RIGHT Lengths of fine mosquito netting waft gently on an on-shore breeze through the windows of this airy bedroom on the island of Lamu, off the east coast of Africa.

In my blue and white bedroom I have used layers of blue and white check curtains and shades with embroidered curtains, all of which can easily be rehung seasonally to create a cool look for summer and a warmer winter atmosphere.

Fine bed linen is seen by some as a luxury and by others, including myself, as an essential. Historically, traditional linen lost popularity during the years of post-war austerity when lack of household staff and reduced circumstances forced people to look for cheaper and easier alternatives. Experiments with synthetic fibers resulted in sheets that never wrinkled but equally did not breathe – a very uncomfortable experience. However, from about 1970 onward, there has been a gradual move away from man-made fibres back to natural cottons and linens and a great resurgence in the popularity of antique linen. This began in the 1960s and '70s, largely thanks to the hippie movement which started the craze for buying old clothes, partly because they were fun and anti-establishment, and partly because they could be picked up for a song. The fascination with old clothes progressed to include old linen, lace, and textiles. Today, every house sale and clearance that reveals a cache of old linen draws in eager buyers, enthusiasts for the past who are aware that old linen represents wonderful value for money. To re-create the same quality and fine workmanship today would be prohibitively expensive.

Today, modern technology and the manufacture of easy-care cottons have brought good-quality bed linen within the reach of many people for whom monogrammed, handstitched pure Irish linen sheets are out of the question. (Though I have to admit that personally, as I have already said, I rank crisp, newly laundered linen sheets high on my list of priorities.) America led the world in developing easy-care, reasonably priced, pure cotton bed linen and it is still the market leader. However, there is new competition from countries such as China and Indonesia where skilled embroiderers are now producing beautifully decorated bed linen in the same way that earlier generations produced export ware porcelain.

ABOVE The gold fern finials were actually taken from an old mirror – all that was needed was a little re-touching in flat gold paint. The natural form of the leaves works well with the soft fabric of the drapes, and adds a subtle grandeur, reflected in the gold motifs on the roman shade.

RIGHT These blue and white drapes define the shape of the bay window recess. The larger pattern in the foreground and the smaller check close to the balcony make the recess appear deeper, creating a wonderful contrast between the bold blues and soft light streaming into the bedroom.

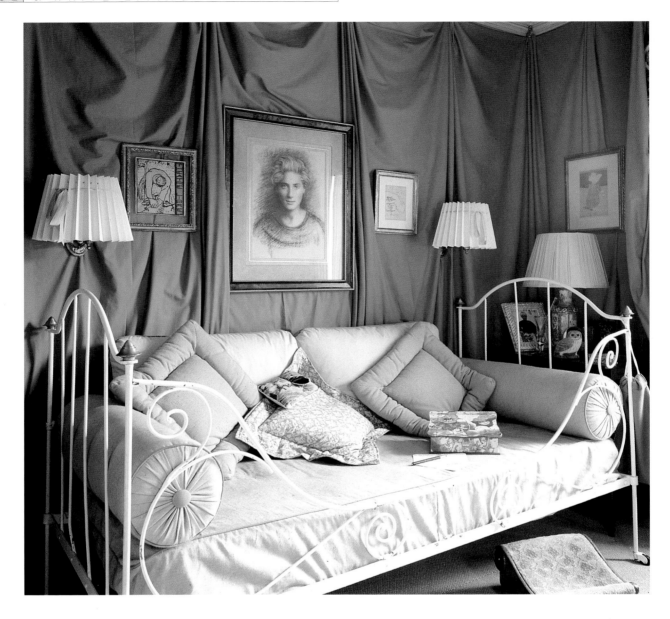

ABOVE An antique French day
bed, painted white, occupies one
end of this small country study.
The room has been canopied
with inexpensive blue cotton, and
the pictures and objects, chosen
for their decorative effect,
perpetuate the blue theme.

RIGHT This airy bedroom is
dominated by an imposing
four-poster bed built of local
mahogany, the height of its
posts accentuated by swathes
of fine mosquito netting. The
sculptural quality of the empty
chair on the bare cedar floor is
enhanced by its faded peeling
blue paint.

ABOVE LEFT Capturing the theme of blue and white to perfection, two Chinese vases have been transformed into lamp bases and placed on toile-covered tables on either side of the bed.

BELOW LEFT A collection of blue and white china is displayed on a blue iron stand with glass shelves. The cream and blue chair softens the overall effect and complements the cream bed covering.

RIGHT This elegant bedroom shows an inspired mixing of a blue and white toile fabric for the walls and curtains, highlighted with paintings and prints of Chinese bowls and vases. The addition of real blue and white porcelain is a clever touch which helps create a perfect room.

In terms of decoration, the traditional French toile bedroom still epitomizes true blue and white for me. The scenes of pastoral idyll have a romantic beauty to them which is perfect for use in the bedroom. The same toile is used for the curtains, headboard, bed skirt, and bed cover and is even battened onto the walls. It also appears in any upholstery such as a chaise longue, stool or armchair. It is used uninhibitedly throughout and the pattern runs uninterrupted from one side of the room to the other and from floor to ceiling (sometimes that is covered, too). Woodwork is usually painted flat off-white or gray. Many companies now produce matching toile fabric and wallpaper which makes this scheme far easier to re-create.

ABOVE One of the bedrooms at the Shaker village of Hancock in New Hampshire. The beds are narrow and a thick string is used instead of springs to support the sleeper. An unused chair is stored on pegs on a wooden pegboard around the room, along with other objects and a rail for hanging towels.

LEFT The small window of this attic bedroom is dwarfed by the white iron bedstead and there is a playful glimpse of blue and white striped undersheet between the lacy valance and matching cotton cover.

There are many other interpretations of the romantic bedroom. To some it may be soft blue walls, billowing sprigged muslin curtains, and a traditional Victorian iron bed covered with eyelet linen. Others may prefer a contemporary look using bold patterns on walls and drapes softened by white lace on the bed. For a romantic look the light should be diffuse, filtered through fabric or shutters.

Muslin, eyelet, dotted Swiss, and pretty laces are fabrics that enable highly decorative and very feminine effects to be created around windows and over beds. Accents of blue can be added in the trimmings and tie-backs, in the linen, or simply in the arrangements of pictures, china, and decorative objects.

87

RIGHT Two 18th-century French ceramic lions by Lunneville recline under the finely cut French bed linen and a blue periwinkle Northumberland quilt.

OPPOSITE A length of white cotton nailed across the window and caught with a thin band of braid and beads serves as a curtain, its ethereal quality exaggerated by the huge heavy tassels that hang as ornamentation on either side. The walls of this bedroom are lightly washed with blue and several checked rugs of different sizes and tones of blue cover the blue tiled floor.

How you choose to decorate your room will inevitably be influenced by where you live. Cool tiled floors, walls colorwashed chalky blue, and shuttered windows are perfect for a hot climate but can feel distinctly chilly somewhere cooler; whereas fabric-lined walls, quilted headboards and thick carpets are appropriate for a cold climate but would seem stifling in the tropics. Although heating and air-conditioning can now protect us from the extremes of climate and mean that we can introduce elements of a favorite style of decoration regardless of where we live, it is still not advisable to wholly defy our location – a room decorated in such a manner will be a conversation topic for a short while, but will soon pall.

Although a carpet is not always appropriate, a rug is always welcome next to the bed – even the Shakers, with their pared-down lifestyle, saw this as a necessity rather than a luxury. Rugs are wonderfully decorative objects which can look marvelous in a blue and white bedroom whether laid on a tiled floor, on polished wooden floorboards, or on top of a soft wool carpet.

In other parts of the house it is usually necessary to bear in mind practical considerations, but in the bedroom I feel that these matters should be forgotten. If a cream carpet strewn with fragile, but beautiful rugs is your heart's desire then so be it; or if your mind strays towards a velvet-covered chaise longue piled high with cushions on which you may one day find the time to recline and read novels; this is your own private retreat and you should do exactly as you wish. Your bedroom should be a place that allows you to leave behind the usual concerns of daily life, a place of relaxation and quiet reflection which allows you to emerge refreshed and invigorated.

Central to the bedroom is the bed. We spend, on average, a third of our lives in bed, yet it is quite extraordinary just how many people sleep in an uncomfortable bed. Buy the best bed you can afford – a beautifully decorated bedroom filled with wonderful objects should be conducive to restful sleep and must include a comfortable bed. The decor will be of little consolation if you are tossing and turning.

ABOVE Twin beds festooned with mosquito netting and covered with a simple blue and white cotton bedspread make this guest room look cool and inviting.

LEFT 18th-century paneling in this French chateau has been painted a classical "gris tendre." The niche bed, draped in an unusual way, has a secret door in its back wall that opens onto the bathroom.

In your lovely blue and white bedroom do make sure that you haven't forgotten the mundane practicalities that ease everyday life. A dressing table should be positioned near a window so that you can apply your makeup in good natural light, and should also be well-illuminated at night, but this need not mean strong light – low-wattage light bulbs tinted in warm shades are far more flattering to the complexion and will do wonders for your confidence. Sockets for appliances such as hairdryers should be easily accessible and positioned near the dressing table. Lovely old mirrors are perfect for the bedroom, with their aged silvering they reflect beautifully soft images which enhance both yourself and your room.

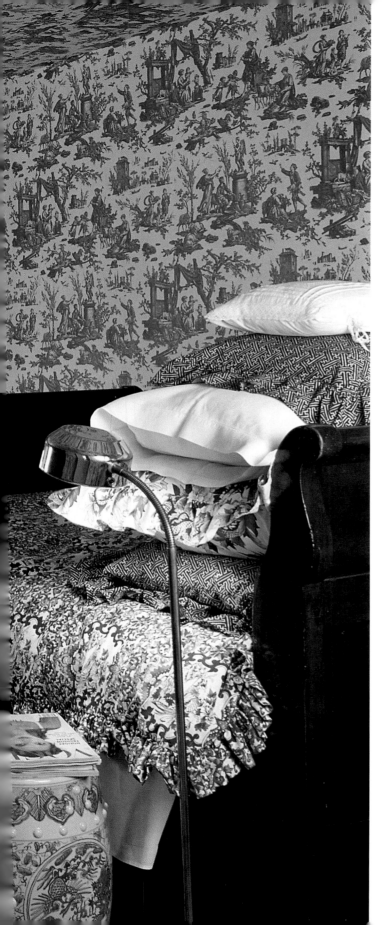

LEFT Designer Mimmi
O'Connell describes her
bedrooms as boxes and this
one is nicknamed "the teapot."
Cocooned in a blue and white
toile de Jouy paper that covers
both walls and ceiling, the bed
is piled high with alternating
blue and white pillows. Canvas
shades, rolled halfway, are
tied with contrasting fabric
that matches the striped
dress curtains.

Because the bedroom is essentially a nighttime room
it is vital that careful thought is given to its lighting.
A central overhead light is seldom necessary or
advisable as it tends to shed harsh light and leaves
you exposed to the glare of bare light bulbs as you lie
in your bed. It is far better to have soft pools of light
that illuminate only the immediate surroundings and
lend the room an air of mystery and romance. Candles
will give the softest light of all but most of us save
them for very special occasions – daily use would be far
too hazardous. Table lamps are ideal for either side of
the bed, as are wall lights on articulated arms which can
be set low on the wall behind. Off-white or cream
pleated shades will glow with a soft light which is
flatteringly diffuse, while dark blue lampshades will
throw dramatic arcs of light downward, creating deep
shadows around them.

If a more general light is essential, uplights can be
used to throw light up onto the ceiling and reflect it
softly downward, especially when they are fitted with
dimmer switches, which give you very flexible control of
the lighting levels. Similarly, an old crystal chandelier,
in all its decorative beauty, can look magnificent in
a bedroom, but once again, it is essential that it is
fitted with a dimmer switch or the light will be far
too dazzling.

During the day, cream shades can be used at the
windows to filter out the harsher rays of sunlight while
still allowing a warm and diffuse light through.

93

PAGE 94 In this London bedroom designed by Anne Singer, toile walls, curtains, and headboard contrast pleasingly with the military precision of the pillows and the superb indigo bedspread.

PAGE 95 This blue and white bedroom in New York also uses blue and white toile on the walls, but as the backdrop for a pair of large Chinese watercolors and antique white bed linen, the effect is quite different.

ABOVE A tiny bedroom on Juliette Mole's former houseboat which was moored on the Thames in London. The bed is scattered with pillows and it doubles as a day bed and work area.

RIGHT The shelves of an Austrian cupboard are stacked with an assortment of fabric and linen, beautifully starched and ironed. Pomanders and muslin bags filled with lavender keep the cupboard smelling sweet.

Storage is an important element in any bedroom. It is essential to have ample wardrobe and drawer space to keep your clothes looking their best and to allow easy access. A pretty armoire is decorative but seldom spacious enough for your needs. In a toile de Jouy bedroom, hanging space would be concealed by covering closet doors with the same fabric as used on the walls. This type of "hidden" storage is a good way of keeping a room looking uncluttered. Space permitting, of course, a walk-in closet is the ideal solution, but it is also nice to display some of your more decorative possessions. A hat collection can look as good as a group of pictures on a wall and a glass-fronted cupboard shows off neatly folded linens.

FIVE

BATHING IN
BLUE &
WHITE

LEFT A bathroom in Piers von
Westenholz's country house is lined with
tongue-and-groove paneling and has been
painted blue throughout. A double basin
and a set of ivory-backed brushes add
a touch of grandeur.

O F ALL THE ROOMS IN THE HOUSE IT SEEMS
that blue and white is least often associated
with the bathroom. Perhaps this is because it is
not considered a warm and cozy combination; it may
also be because traditional marbles are more often pink
or green in tone, and color schemes evolved from
their coloring. Whatever the reasons, I consider blue
and white to be a stunning color combination
regardless of where it is used – it is as suitable for the
bathroom as any other room in the house. Nowadays,
with good heating and plentiful hot water, cool colors
can be used freely.

It is interesting to note that, historically, blue did
feature in the original built-in bathrooms. Early toilets
were decorated both inside and out with colorful
designs. The bowls were printed or painted with a
variety of fruit, flower, or willow patterns before being
glazed; blue was a popular color as were red and pink.
These elaborate pieces are now much sought-after
antiques and can still be found, together with their
original water tanks.

99

With the increased popularity of the more traditional style of bathroom fixtures there are antiques dealers and reclamation yards that can supply everything from original faucets and chrome towel rails to extraordinary nineteenth-century shower cubicles which look as if they could have inspired H G Wells's time machine! When renovating an old bathroom or planning a new one it is worthwhile taking the time to visit your local specialists to see what is available. Even if you cannot afford to buy all old fixtures, you can still give your bathroom a historic look by combining one old piece, say a basin, or even just original faucets or old tiles, with modern copies of the old bathroom fittings. Today many manufacturers are even making reproductions of the antique blue and white toilets and basins which will certainly give an authentic touch to traditional-style bathrooms, particularly when paired with a roll-top cast-iron bath on claw feet. Before embarking on a bathroom that includes old fixtures, it is recommended that you find yourself a plumber who is not overwhelmed by the far-from-standard nature of much of the pipework that will be needed to make it function. Although bargains can still be found, a cheap price may indicate there is something wrong or missing. A good plumber will be happy to check over any proposed purchase and give you an idea of the time and expense involved in getting it into working order. This can help you avoid expensive mistakes.

LEFT The decorative theme for this bathroom in a Malibu beach house designed by Dot Spikings would appear to have been inspired by the large painting hanging above the bath. Linen shades and a simple wicker chair complete the picture.

RIGHT A novel storage idea has been introduced in this bathroom, where two rows of beautifully ironed shirts hang from a rail designed like a type of scaffolding.

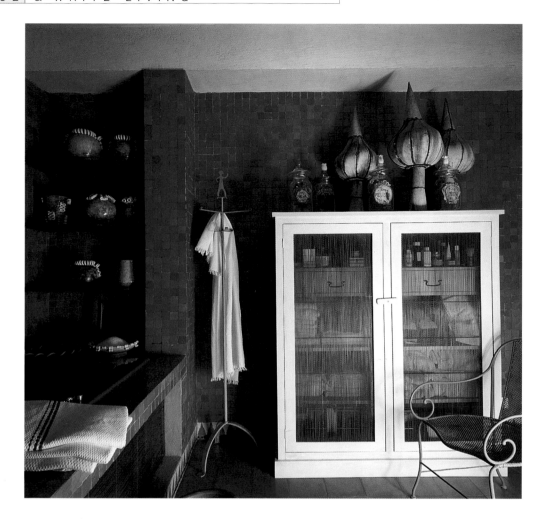

LEFT AND RIGHT A mixture of different tiles is used to theatrical effect in this Italian bathroom. The narrow entrance is visually enhanced with a tile border around the doorway. The walls are decorated with glazed tiles of irregular hues of blue and continuity throughout the apartment is maintained by the floor tiles. Spartan rather than comfortable, the bathroom is furnished with only an iron chair and a towel stand, both painted a pale verdigris.

After a rather unfortunate detour into colored bathroom suites in the 1960s and '70s, many people have returned to the safety of white bathroom fixtures. I find that even the simplest all-white bathroom can be given a new lease on life just by adding a blue glass, china, towels, and fabrics. For instance, a contemporary bathroom can be given a very fresh, summery look with accessories and towels in forget-me-not blue, billowing white muslin curtains, a glass vase of seasonal blue and white flowers, and a painted cane chair with plump cushions upholstered in a pretty striped fabric.

Most modern bathrooms are very compact and a major improvement can be made by the provision of additional space, or even the illusion of space. If you are

someone who always prefers a shower, and yet a large part of the bathroom is taken up by a bath, you should consider removing it and installing a luxurious tiled shower. There are wonderful handmade tiles in rich shades of blue which, when mixed together, have all the opulence of a traditional Turkish bath. If you are unwilling to sacrifice your bath you can still create a feeling of space by replacing one or, even better, two tiled walls with mirrors. The resulting reflections will create an enormously increased sense of space. Like tiles, mirrors can be drilled using a special drill bit which will allow you to mount lights on these walls and glass shelves for storage and display. Use soft lighting, however, or the effect will be too dazzling.

LEFT A wonderful collection of blue and white porcelain handles and chains circa 1890 demonstrates how practically anything looks more decorative when shown "en masse."

RIGHT Patriotism has taken hold of this bathroom decorated in memory of Queen Victoria. The shagpile carpet has been designed to resemble the British flag and the walls are adorned with a mixed assortment of prints and memorabilia. A bronze bust of Queen Victoria stands on a stripped pine column.

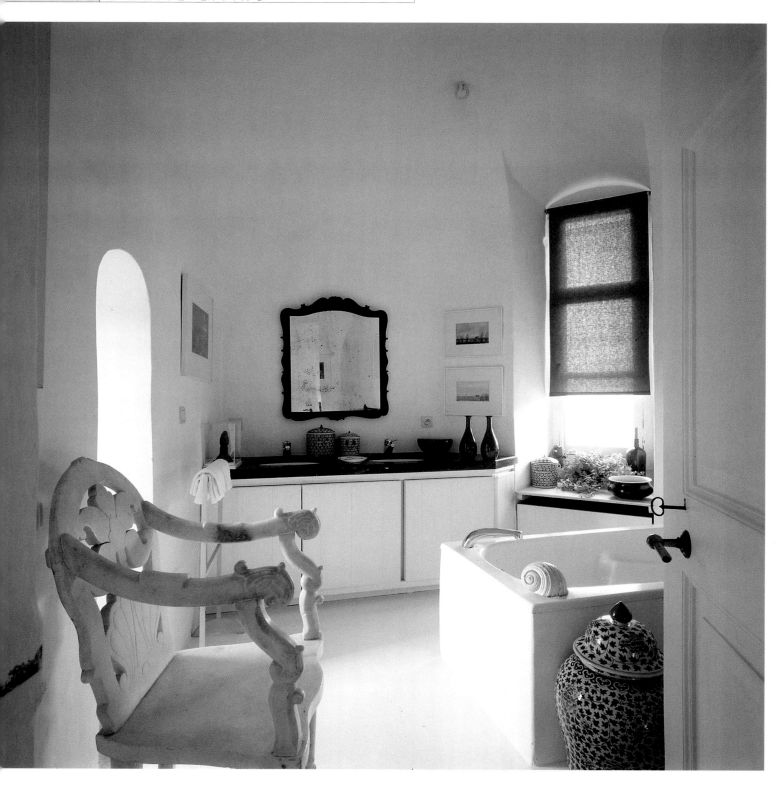

LEFT A tranquil white bathroom in Axel Vervoordt's castle. A carved marble armchair dominates an otherwise simple bathroom and subtle touches of pale and dark blue contribute to the simple air of elegance of this room.

ABOVE RIGHT Hand-appliquéd cotton trim on cotton bath towels from the Monogrammed Linen Shop in London.

CENTER RIGHT Hand-embroidered monograms and a scallop-shaped edging give towels a decorative finish.

BELOW RIGHT Go for a homemade effect by simply tying bundles of towels together.

Just as the furnished look has become popular in kitchens, the furnished style is increasingly favored in bathrooms and is wonderfully suited to a blue and white theme. For it to work well, you do need a reasonably large bathroom or you are in danger of sacrificing function on the altar of style. If you are converting an adjoining bedroom into a bathroom, this is a style to consider as it has much more the appearance of a comfortable living space than does a more conventional bathroom.

For a bathroom with a country look, floorboards can be uncovered and scattered with cotton rugs, and tongue-and-groove boarding fastened to the walls and painted hyacinth blue. With an antique pine blanket rack to store towels, a comfortable chair, and a roll-top bath on feet positioned centrally against one wall, the bathroom becomes a retreat to linger in and enjoy.

If a richer, warmer look is more to your taste, you could consider using an antique or reproduction blue and white toilet and basin with dark polished mahogany fixtures accompanied by a bath with a matching mahogany surround. With deep blue paintwork, a patterned wallpaper, lots of pictures on the wall, and a thick carpet you have all the ingredients for a traditional bathroom full of creature comforts. Further enhance the mood with draped curtains at the windows looped back to reveal shutters or shades. These combine to keep the light level low, as will the use of shaded light fittings.

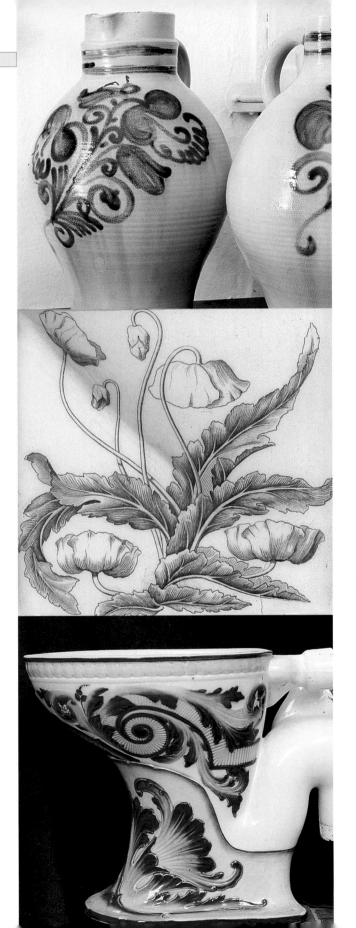

ABOVE LEFT Natural blues often evoke a Mediterranean feel — here, the colors appear barely dry, running along the clay ridges of hand-painted pots. Placed near a rough plaster wall, this makes for an intriguing mix of creams and whites.

CENTER LEFT The painterly quality of this blue linework on porcelain has elegance and sophistication, and works well alongside the naive pattern of the pots. Although the styles appear opposite, the curves of both flower motifs are a vivid, sensuous combination.

BELOW LEFT An example of the wide variety of decorative finishes available in toilets during the late 19th century.

RIGHT A wonderful group of antique blue and white toilets dating from 1880–1905. During that time seventy-five per cent of all bathroom fittings were blue and white.

LEFT A Victorian canopy shower-bath painted a brilliant powder blue is both highly decorative and very practical. The screen is no longer necessary to keep drafts at bay but can create areas of privacy within a modern bathroom.

One of my favorite luxuries in my bathroom is an ample supply of thick, fluffy, white towels warmed on a heated rail – nothing is more inviting. In fact I consider good-quality towels a necessity, not a luxury, but I do like to ring the changes for different effects: blue monograms on white towels or white monograms on blue towels, or sometimes a white bath sheet topped with a hand towel and face cloth in blue, or vice versa. A good selection of blue and white towels in varying sizes will allow you to change the mood of your bathroom in an instant. Picture an all-white bathroom and how different it looks when plain blue towels are used instead of white. As all blues blend well and there is no fear of making a mistake, you can use three or four different blues graded from dark to light on the same towel rail, and your extra towels will look pretty piled on a shelf tied up with a checked blue and white ribbon.

One of the ways we judge a good hotel is by the quality of its bathroom and the accompanying towels, robes, and toiletries. A windowless box with thin towels and cheap soap will not be memorable, but a light airy bathroom with a plentiful supply of lovely towels, luxurious bathrobes, and fine-quality toiletries is an experienced to be savored. Take note of the things you particularly enjoy and introduce them to your own bathroom. In particular, the best hotels seem to find bathrobes that are longer, thicker and more absorbent than usual. Treat yourself to one from the hotel (they are usually for sale) or buy one from a reputable maker. Buy the biggest robe you can find, as they will always shrink when laundered and a robe is far better too big than too small.

Fine soap and fragrant bath oils add immeasurably to the pleasures and satisfaction of the bath. Don't wait to be given them, buy them for yourself – it is after all, a modest indulgence.

ABOVE A wonderful array of towels, piled high on an antique wooden blanket rack. The large oil painting of a grandmother and two children gives exactly the right feel to this small space. People are often frightened to use large paintings in small spaces, but doing so actually increases the feeling of space.

111

SIX

BLUE & WHITE COLLECTIONS

LEFT Interior decorator Roger Banks-Pye of Britain's Colefax and Fowler was an enthusiastic collector of anything blue and white. From Chinese porcelain to enamel mugs, the shelves in his kitchen almost buckle under their combined weight.

I HAVE ALWAYS LOVED BLUE AND WHITE porcelain and I believe that more than anything else it epitomizes the extraordinary allure of these colors. Although these pages do show some serious collections of porcelain, built up over the years by expert collectors, the joy of blue and white is that it can cater for all tastes and pockets. You can put your name down with an antiques dealer and gradually build up an entire dinner service or you can pick up pieces here and there and put together a wonderful harlequin set. You can enjoy priceless jardinières and pots that are valuable investments or you can salvage broken pitchers or chipped bowls to use as flower pots and vases – worthless in commercial terms, but much loved and treasured objects in daily use.

All of us enjoy the "hunt," wandering through street markets and fairs, browsing in antiques shops and bazaars in the hope of finding a little bit of blue and white china which may or may not be valuable, but which will certainly enhance a room. Once your eye is attuned to blue and white, you will find it everywhere.

113

If you are prepared to buy damaged or repaired blue and white china, you will find pieces for next to nothing that would be worth a fortune undamaged. You can still enjoy the pleasure of ownership with none of the anxieties and responsibilities. A piece which, in perfect condition, would be locked away in a display cupboard, can be in daily use. Find alternative uses for chipped china – I use pitchers as vases with the flowers artfully arranged to hide the chips. Sugar bowls make ideal plant bowls and big bowls can be planted up with bulbs, the earth covered with green moss. Vegetable dishes that have lost their lids also make good planters, and odd saucers are perfect stands for pots and vases to protect the table underneath.

ABOVE In a small hallway of my home I have arranged a geometric display of my antique tea caddies under framed groups of off-white intaglio prints. The contrast between the two collections is visually very interesting.

RIGHT A traditional Chinese red lacquered display cabinet, with two small drawers beneath one of the shelves painted with charming flowers, holds a collection of Mimmi O'Connell's blue and white ginger jars and Chinese pots.

LEFT Above a traditional mahogany side-table laden with family silver, narrow shelves at one end of this formal dining room display a set of plates decorated with handpainted flowers.

The history of blue and white china is a long and fascinating story, and like many other collectors, I was enormously excited by the discovery of the fabulous Chinese porcelain cargoes that have been rescued from the bottom of the sea over the last decade. The Nanking Cargo was the first to be salvaged, and the press and public alike were fascinated by this tale of shipwreck on the high seas, the lure of the East, and the amazing dedication and skill of salvage expert Captain Michael Hatcher and his team. Prior to the sale at Christie's in Amsterdam on April 28th, 1986, record crowds lined up patiently to view the sale, and people who had never previously ventured into an auction house joined the bidding in order to acquire for themselves a tiny piece of this remarkable history. There were bidders from all around the world for the 160,000 pieces of blue and white porcelain which were auctioned over five days, and the final tally far exceeded the original estimates.

RIGHT Forgoing the formality of a laid table, assorted Chinese plates are stacked in readiness for a buffet. Crisp white linen napkins are tied with a length of dark blue ribbon and flatware is upended in a pretty Chinese bowl.

PAGE 118 China perfectly positioned on a hutch is one of the most traditional but still most successful ways of displaying such objects.

PAGE 119 A display of blue and white china in front of a painting of the same subject. It may seem obsessive, but is very effective and gives the room real style.

LEFT One wall of Lebanese decorator Jo Thome's bedroom in Beirut is lined with pale blue shelves stretching from floor to ceiling. They house Thome's collection of blue and white china displayed with no apparent themes.

ABOVE AND RIGHT A Regency bookcase containing collections of vellum books, Bristol Blue glass, Chinese crackleware, and powder blue glaze vases. This combination of books and objects is seen through the crystal drops of a 19th-century Venetian chandelier.

LEFT Ceramics of different periods and styles reflect changes in pattern and density of color. The top plate is a modern design from Mexico, its dark color contrasting with the paler, more intricate Chinese design of the earlier 19th-century meat plate. The bowl is an early Turkish ceramic.

RIGHT, CLOCKWISE FROM ABOVE LEFT An 18th-century Chinese teapot with asparagus handles from my collection; a group of large jardinières made of enameled iron by Paris & Compagnie, France, in 1860; a Ming design, Chieng Lung-period temple jar holding rolls of old parchment; a 19th-century splatterware pitcher on a garden table ready to be filled with white daisies.

Romance, mystery, and adventure all play their part in the worldwide fascination and perennial attraction of blue and white porcelain. From the earliest examples which made the hazardous journey to Europe in the fourteenth and fifteenth centuries – rare and precious Ming vases which were available to only the wealthiest and most dedicated collectors – the love affair with blue and white has never waned.

The original outbreak of "Chinamania" dates from the seventeenth century. It began, once again, in Amsterdam in 1604, when the cargo of a Portuguese trading ship was put up for auction. Captured en route from China, the cargo consisted of some hundred thousand "porcelains" and its sale caused as much of a stir as did its Nanking successor almost four hundred years later. It stimulated so much demand that soon all the East India companies began trading in porcelain, most of which was blue and white.

In England Charles II made tea-drinking fashionable after he was given a small packet of it as a wedding present. Cups, saucers, teapots, and caddies as well as jars, urns, garden tubs, jardinières, fish bowls, molds, pitchers, mugs, and dessert and dinner services were all made in abundance for the European market. Within fifty years Chinese porcelain had been transformed from a rare and precious collector's prize to readily available everyday tableware and decorative objects, painted with patterns that were specifically designed for European tastes. Blue and white was here to stay.

LEFT An extremely rare collection of French 17th-century knives with blue and white porcelain handles in their original box.

RIGHT A remarkable collection of Chieng Lung tea jars and canisters, circa 1706–1797. The jars are exceptionally large and are very rare in these sizes. Originally they would all have had ceramic lids, but with the passage of time most of these have been broken and replaced with wooden or silver ones.

It was not long before European manufacturers, jealous of the success of Chinese export porcelain, looked to cash in on the market. State manufacturers in France, Italy, and Germany tried their best to emulate the Chinese. The closest in appearance was the tin-glazed earthenware produced in, and now synonymous with, the Dutch town of Delft. The Bow factory in England, known as New Canton, was making blue and white porcelain from 1747 and its early chinoiserie-inspired designs are now exceptionally rare collectors' pieces.

By the 1770s, the English potters of North Staffordshire had perfected the art of transfer-printing in blue on earthenware, a much less expensive material than porcelain. Josiah Spode led the way, helped by fine craftsmen such as Thomas Minton. Domestic production gradually increased, helped by the fashion for tea-drinking and by a wartime duty levied on silver which fostered a demand for pottery teapots. By 1799, the tax on imported porcelain stood at 109 per cent, and more and more people turned to companies such as Caughley and Spode for both new dinner services and replacements and additions copied from the original Chinese designs. The ubiquitous Willow pattern created by Spode dates from the early years of the 19th century. Just as European blue and white developed directly from its oriental counterpart, so designs can be traced from East to West and back again in a fascinating international circle.

The first period of blue and white printed pottery in England was wholly Chinese-influenced, with innovative artists and engravers such as Thomas Davis, Thomas Lucas, Thomas Minton, and John Ainsworth all drawing their inspiration from fine Chinese ceramics already imported into Britain. As skills and techniques developed, a gradual "Europeanization" took place and a practiced eye can detect a Dutch-style "Chinese" house or willow tree, or spot a Palladian arch on a Chinese pagoda.

Blue and white is a theme which has entranced ceramic artists the world over. The Middle East, probably Baluchistan, was the source of the cobalt used by the 14th-century Chinese potters and the range of this precious commodity can be seen in the vivid blues of tiles and pottery throughout the Islamic world, stretching across North Africa and on to Moorish Spain. The Topkapi Museum in Istanbul has one of the finest collections of Chinaware, brought back from China by camel trains for use by wealthy Turks and Persians who traded cargoes of cobalt in exchange.

From the blue and white tiles and tulipieres of Dutch Delft to the Willow and Wedgwood of England and on through time and place to the brilliant hues of modern Provençal pottery and Spanish faïence, the lure of collecting blue and white china is universal. It remains as fresh and appealing today as it ever was, and it is little wonder that those salvaged cargoes of precious porcelain remain so attractive.

ABOVE Detail from a blue and white enameled iron Paris jardinière from Guinievere Antiques, London.

RIGHT An extremely rare collection of "half-jugs." These were used as traveler's samples in the 19th century.

A good collection of blue and white tiles can be a fascinating document of the history and development of blue and white porcelain as well as a decorative delight. Intensely glazed Chinese tiles, the beautiful geometric patterns on Middle Eastern tiles, the soft hues of the Dutch Delft ware, and the Moorish design of Spanish and Portuguese tiles are incredibly diverse in color and origin, yet blend harmoniously into a glorious and complete picture.

ABOVE Examples of modern tiles available from the Delft factory in Holland. Keeping to the original 17th-century themes, each tile depicts a figure, an animal, or an object.

RIGHT A mosaic of antique tiles, some Delft, from The Water Monopoly, London.

LEFT A row of burnished copper saucepans and their lids hang from hooks against a wall lined with assorted blue and white tiles in one corner of this Majorcan kitchen. Two local pottery bowls on a rough stone work surface are used for storing wooden spoons and utensils – their venerability is evident from the number of staples with which they are held together.

RIGHT Two details of the tiled floor of a Burmese temple in the Saigan Hills near Mandalay show contrasting themes along the same basic design.

Of course porcelain is only one area of blue and white collecting – there is much, much more to explore. On my list of "collectables" in blue and white are blue glass candlesticks, vases, and scent bottles; any objects in blue stone or marble, such as lapis lazuli or similar (the exact material does not matter, it is the color that counts). Also blue glass and clear glass "drops" from old chandeliers which look so pretty when mixed together in a bowl or plate; tall, thin celery vases filled with blue glass beads; and blue "witches' balls" and decorative porcelain objects including tea caddies, ginger jars, and teapots. I collect pure white china in the form of figurines, candlesticks, and plates – they look wonderful on a shelf or tabletop or accompanying a table setting of blue and white.

There is a jewel-like quality to blue glass which makes it irresistible to the blue and white collector. Artistic glass-making had its beginnings in thirteenth century Venice since which time the best glass makers have produced wonderful examples of their craft in a range of blues, from a stunning deep blue to a wonderful opalescent turquoise. The Venetians guarded their secrets closely for nearly 300 years and it was not until this secrecy was relaxed that the techniques and skills could spread to other countries in Europe. Inspired by the Venetians, the Germans and Bohemians soon developed a fine glass industry of their own. The Bohemians, although best known for their ruby red glass, were also producing a rich transparent blue glass which was achieved by adding cobalt to the formula. The eighteenth century saw the arrival of fine glass-making in England, and the wine glasses of the time are unsurpassed in quality – particularly prized are glasses with color twist stems. Among the makers of colored glass the most famous were based in Bristol, who produced a deep blue glass of wonderful quality known as Bristol Blue. This is much sought after by collectors – a collection of Bristol Blue is quite breathtakingly beautiful; it is a great favorite of mine and I have a number of pieces in my home. Although old pieces are increasingly rare and expensive, Bristol Blue is still being made so it is not too late to start a collection of this lovely glass.

131

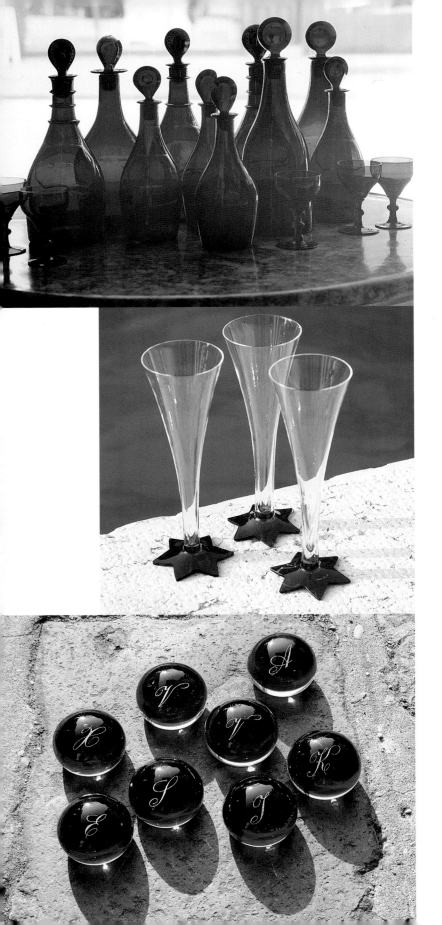

LEFT Examples of the versatility of glass available from the Murano Glass Factory in Venice. A collection of blue glass bottles of various sizes with ornate stoppers (top left). Up-to-the-minute champagne flutes with jaunty blue bases (center). A collection of monogrammed paper weights (below left).

RIGHT A modern art or fantasy mask. This hair-raising sculpture stands in isolation in a large white entrance hall, ready to shock all who enter.

Today there are many contemporary craftsmen and women who are making beautiful decorative objects in blue and white, and this is a source of "collectables" that should not be ignored. It is all too easy to neglect the modern in favor of the old, but modern craftsmen rely on their patrons just as much as did their predecessors, so, if we wish to keep these skills alive we must support them. If you find someone whose work you admire, such as a potter, ceramicist, sculptor, or glass-maker, consider commissioning them to make something for you. Most artists enjoy working this way – making an item for a specific individual and a certain location – and you will find that there is a particular pleasure in owning something which has been made just for you. Put your name on the mailing lists of your local contemporary galleries which show high-quality crafts and you will be invited to previews where you will have a chance to buy and also talk to the artist. It could be the beginning of a fruitful relationship.

Even if your interest is mainly for the old you will find that modern china, glass and accessories can look marvelous interspersed among a collection of antiques.

LEFT A pair of Bristol Blue jugs
stand on the granite work
surface in a corner of my
kitchen. The large one, a
present from my son Michael,
is the biggest we have
ever seen.

How you choose to display your blue and white collectables is just as important as the collection itself – the finest porcelain will be overlooked if it is dusty and ill-lit, whilst an inexpensive but pretty collection of blue and white can look deceptively important when arranged with flair.

I love mixing many different patterns of blue and white together as I find this makes for a charming informality, but I equally appreciate the dramatic effect that can be achieved by displaying just one important piece in a room, especially when it is carefully lit. Lighting is all important – an alcove lit by subtle, diffuse light will display collectables far better than the dark interior of a glass-fronted cupboard.

A small collection of decorative objects looks larger if it is arranged on shelves with a mirror backing, and in a small room this will also give the illusion of more space. A hutch is one of the prettiest ways to display china, but where space is limited, use a wall-hung plate rack; there are some wonderful old country pieces in fruitwood or you could have one custom made to fit the available space exactly.

One of the most effective ways to display glass is on glass shelves in front of a window. The light coming through the window gives the glass so much more life and clarity than when displayed against a solid, unreflective background. Keep the shelf supports to a minimum and your glass collectables will appear as if suspended in mid-air.

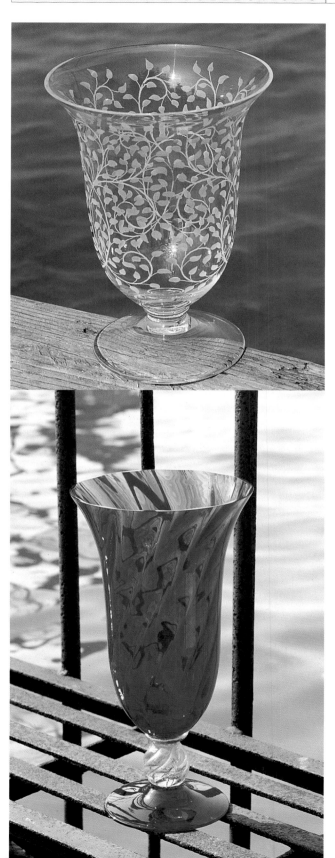

BELOW Detail of the mother-of-pearl inlay on a chest of drawers at the Sursock Palace in Beirut. The ceramic handle is designed to resemble the iris of a human eye.

ABOVE, ABOVE RIGHT, BELOW RIGHT Dark blue glasses of various sizes are designed with matching glass plates in a harlequin pattern, some clear versions are elaborately engraved, while others are elegantly shaped.

135

SEVEN

BLUE & WHITE FABRICS

LEFT A selection of tickings is a marvellous example of the simple beauty of blue and white fabrics. Originally used to cover mattresses, this crisp and hard-wearing fabric is now used for everything from curtains to upholstery.

BLUE AND WHITE FABRICS ARE IN A CLASS OF their own. No other color combination has quite the same magical effect and whether it be stripes or checks, toiles or chintzes, linens or damasks, almost every pattern looks better in blue and white. Although the appeal of blue and white is, in some ways, quite mysterious and unquantifiable, it is, nevertheless, a commercially recognized fact. Publishers have discovered that a blue and white cover picture on an interior design magazine will always sell much more successfully than any other color combination. Possibly this is because blue and white fabrics have never been out of fashion. They are multi-dimensional: they look fresh and crisp by day, and evocative and beautiful at night; they range from the most mundane of fabrics – coarse-textured ticking stripes, dishcloth cottons and gingham checks – to the most exotic of fine silks, damasks, and embroideries. From the deepest midnight-blue velvets through to the flimsiest white muslins and laces, there is truly something here to suit everyone.

137

FAR LEFT The fabrics piled high on these shelves are all antique – batik, toile de Jouy, ticking, floral, checked, striped, and plain – 19th-century versions of the blue and white theme which was as popular then as it is today.

LEFT Linen embroidered with blue monograms. A simple way of copying this is to use a transfer alphabet as a pattern and then cross stitch one's own initials onto a plain linen pillow case or towel.

ABOVE Fresh and crisp, blue and white checks are perfect for table linen. There is a wide variety of patterns to choose from and you can use either a single or a variety of designs in your room.

Historically, blue and white fabrics have existed ever since woven cloth was first made. Weaving was a skill which developed alongside the domestication of animals and the cultivation of plants. Although the primary reason these early people made cloth was to provide warmth and protection from the elements, it was not long before dyes were being used for decoration. The earliest cloths were laid out on south-facing slopes to whiten in the sun, while indigo, a pigment extracted from the anil plant, was one of the earliest dyes. The oldest surviving examples of textile printing date from the fifth and sixth centuries BC, but records from tombs and other historic monuments show that printed fabric was around, astonishingly, from as early as 2500BC.

ABOVE A bold design of a full-blown rose.

LEFT A collection of printed and woven fabrics, all with exuberant and abstract patterns. These can add a modern note to a traditional room.

RIGHT A collection of throws and a bag all made with Pierre Frey fabrics hang on Shaker-style hooks in the hall of a seaside home. This illustrates how visually effective different blue and white fabrics can be when hung together.

Rather as the blue and white porcelain of the East inspired new techniques and new patterns in the West, so the brightly colored printed cottons, or calicoes, of India had a dramatic influence on European fabrics. First introduced by the English East India Company and its Dutch counterpart in the early years of the seventeenth century, these cloths were immediately very popular with the public, but less so with the European textile industry. They requested the help of their governments who then moved to protect their own fabrics with restrictions on imports. Not until the middle of the eighteenth century were protective trade bans finally lifted, but their repeal gave rise to one of the most famous of all blue and white fabrics. In 1760,

Christophe Philippe Oberkampf established his printing center at Jouy-en-Josas. His fabrics were printed using copper plates which were larger than the traditional woodblocks and which could be more finely engraved. These first "toiles de Jouy" were usually in blue and white or red and white and depicted pastoral scenes or neo-classical motifs. They rapidly became popular and were used for curtaining and to line walls, as well as for beds and upholstery.

In America, British trade restrictions prevented the mass manufacture of textiles in the colonies until the end of British rule. The earliest examples of European-style decorative weaving from America are blue and white quilted coverlets.

ABOVE A simple and attractive way of storing remnants of fabric is to roll them up and secure them with a length of blue ribbon.

ABOVE RIGHT These toile de Jouy fabrics remain household favorites. Their traditional Arcadian scenes provide a highly decorative touch.

LEFT An amusing and imaginative way of displaying these swatches of blue and white fabric. Their intricate patterns make them appropriate for covering small items.

Today, we accept as normal the extraordinary range of fabrics that is available for us to choose from, but before the Industrial Revolution things were very different. All fabrics were hand-woven and were accordingly cherished as some of the most precious belongings in any household.

The hangings that surrounded a bed were far more valuable than the bed itself. They were seen as the height of opulence, which meant that embroidery and crewel work were seen as suitable aristocratic pastimes.

Blue and white fabrics have featured in one way or another through the centuries right down to the present day. Our own century saw the invention of denim or "de Nimes" fabric, first produced in the town of Nimes in France and without which our modern culture would look quite different. The selection of blue and white fabrics shown on these pages is only a minute fraction of the vast range of contemporary upholstery and curtain fabrics which are available. The range is breathtaking, from the toiles and damasks which pay tribute to the styles of the past and remain enduringly popular, to the freshest of modern checks and stripes. The very diversity of the fabrics shown grouped together helps to illustrate how well blue and white fabrics mesh together. As in the world of nature, all shades of blue seem to tone beautifully, and you will find that using this marvelous combination you can be wonderfully adventurous without the slightest degree of risk.

143

EIGHT

BLUE & WHITE PICTURES

LEFT A work in pastels by Maureen Jordan of a corner of her garden with the ultimate in blue flowers: hydrangeas, lobelia, and pansies. Her paintings always sell out as soon as they come in to my gallery – a tribute to the appeal of my favorites.

I F THE WORLD IS DIVIDED INTO THOSE OF US WHO are passionate about a blue and white way of life and those who are not, then the choice of pictures for such a way of life subdivides us still further. There are, in principle, three very different approaches to selecting works of art.

The first approach is to emphasize the blue and white theme of a room by selecting pictures, paintings or prints which use only these colors both in the artwork and the frames which are also in shades of blue. By layering colors in this way, the room achieves an intense depth of color that is dramatic but welcoming. When I worked with interior designer Stephen Ryan for David Hicks on a bedroom which used this intense approach to choosing pictures for a blue and white room, the watercolors I had commissioned, with their blue rope-twist frames, proved so successful and popular that it led us to produce a series of prints. These prints helped to enable blue and white aficionados all over the world to emulate Stephen Ryan's clean, crisp and dramatic style.

145

ABOVE A delightful painting of a tray set for tea by the Milanese sisters Maris Pia and Marinella Angelini. Paintings like this have always been popular, emitting as they do a feeling of hearth and home.

LEFT Paintings and prints of Chinese Export china are juxtaposed against real pitchers and bowls to accent the color and add depth to the room. What at first glance appears to be shelves laden with blue and white china is, in fact, a kitchen board – a clever trompe l'oeil illusion.

RIGHT A small watercolor of a teapot, cup, and saucer set on a white linen doily in front of a blue and white tiled wall is the perfect painting for a kitchen, especially if it is hung between real china plates.

147

ABOVE This watercolor and gouache painting of pansies in a Nantucket basket by Meg McCarthy explores the variety and richness of the many shades of blue found in the natural world. A perfect foil for a blue and white planter.

LEFT Blue and white containers give gravity to the light, fluffy quality of the parrot tulips in this oil painting by Galley. The gaudiness of their petals makes a clever contrast with the cool blues.

ABOVE RIGHT Nahid Ghodsi's watercolor and gold leaf painting encapsulates both Persian style and western botanical style. The Persian blue gouache frame around the orchid makes it so effective in a blue and white room.

BELOW RIGHT The two watercolors balance the strong background, and make the flowers appear fresh and delicate. The handpainted music paper is a trademark of artist Christine Thouzeau's style.

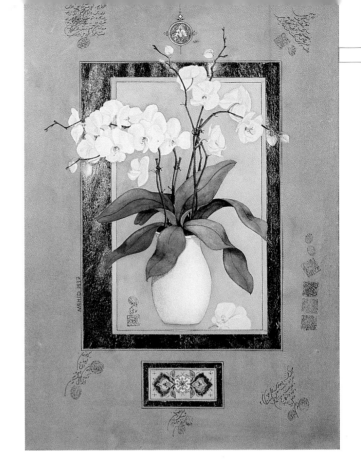

The second approach to choosing pictures for a blue and white room is less obsessive but equally attractive and involves putting together an eclectic and multi-faceted collection of pictures that contain within them an item or items of blue and white: a blue and white bowl filled with flowers; a dash of indigo in a dress; blue flowers in a silver vase or in a landscape; a willow pattern cup and saucer. Your picture may only have a tiny detail in blue, yet within the collection that detail will become a dominant feature and will connect the picture with the rest in a marvelously disparate and unique way. This obviously takes much longer to achieve, but the excitement of the "chase" as you hunt down each individual element is compounded by the effect of the whole collection as it grows.

The third, and possibly the most dramatic, way to choose pictures for a blue and white room, is to ignore the color scheme totally and fill the walls with a rich panoply of oil paintings of all shapes and sizes. I particularly recommend portraits in heavy gilded frames which create an effect which is at once dramatic and richly lustrous. Auction houses can be a good hunting ground for this type of picture, even on a limited budget. A fine portrait by a known artist will rightly command premium prices, but an unsigned picture of a long-forgotten merchant or provincial lady can often be picked up surprisingly cheaply.

Within and around these three differing approaches it can also be effective to intermingle blue and white plates, or other decorative objects, both old and new, among the pictures. This looks extremely attractive in any setting, but is a must when following the second approach. In general there should be some linking theme to the pictures; if not portraits, then choose a subject that appeals to you such as still lifes, wildlife, flowers, or landscapes.

LEFT Collecting themed items in blue and white gives scope for a wonderful range of ephemera. Even the tiniest flash of blue on an antique tea caddy will sit well with a classic country milk pitcher, a fine willow pattern on a tea cup, or an ornate teapot of the deepest hue.

ABOVE Royal blues and golds complement an aqua-marine cameo, and vertical stripes of lemon create a soft, understated effect in this collection of Regency-style artefacts.

BELOW Preserves and their containers can be given the blue and white treatment. Motifs such as hearts, checks, and flowers alternate in blue, white, and yellow with trimmings of lace, cords, and bows.

When deciding on which approach you are going to take when displaying a collection of pictures, it is important not to lose sight of the importance of the content of the pictures themselves. Although you want them to combine in a pleasing totality, each picture should have individual appeal. The pictures should look good next to one another but not be too homogenous – or you may as well use wallpaper. Even if the pictures have a common theme, their style and medium can vary enormously. Detailed watercolors, faded prints, contemporary and period oil paintings can be of related subjects, yet still retain an interesting individuality.

継 其 柳
之 嶼 宗
去 小 元
也 萌
不 芽
意
其

ABOVE In Andras Kaldor's watercolour of the first Eddystone lighthouse, off Plymouth, England, the feeling of shape, sea and sky make it perfect for a blue and white room.

LEFT A little blue and white goes a long way. This screen print of a Chinese chair and porcelain paintbrush holder has just small areas of blue — on the pot, and in a band of flatter pattern, parallel with the chair seat.

ABOVE RIGHT AND BELOW RIGHT Lise Le Coeur's oil paintings depict blue and white Delft tiles with trompe l'oeil. The tickets, envelope and key imposed upon the tiles evoke blue and white as a way of life.

How you choose to mount and frame your pictures will have an enormous effect on how a room looks. Single-color mounts and simple frames will focus the attention on the pictures themselves and can give a room an understated look, whereas mounts embellished with marbled papers and decorative hand-drawn details, surrounded by highly decorative gilded frames, will create a richly opulent atmosphere. Changing the frames on a collection of pictures can dramatically transform them and it is worth taking time and trouble to get the balance right. However, you may find that sometimes oil paintings look best of all with no frame to distract the eye.

When it comes to hanging pictures remember that, unless you are a true professional, achieving straight lines and rigidly symmetrical blocks is fussy and time-consuming work. There are few short cuts, and you will need to measure carefully and lay the pictures out on the floor beforehand. Standing on a chair or stepladder will help you assess the overall effect. A good way of checking if you've got it right is to take a Polaroid – this is a stylist's trick which will allow you to be more objective about the pattern you have created with the pictures. The balance of light and dark, and the overall shape of the display, become more apparent – especially if you look at the photograph upside down! Making adjustments at this stage is much easier than when the pictures are on the wall. Once you are happy with your design and have hung the pictures, you can loosen or tighten the picture wire to alter the height of the picture without the bother of moving the pin. Do not be put off from removing the pins if you need to – pin holes hardly show and it is worth it to achieve the effect you want.

When visiting exhibitions and galleries take note of displays which have been expertly hung and look closely at the mounts and frames and hanging techniques.

If you are to make the most of a collection of pictures, good lighting is as important as the choice of frames and the careful arranging of your display. Whilst a picture light is appropriate for a single important painting, it does not work where a group of pictures are hung together; a single picture light is ineffective and using a light for each picture would be over-bright and messy looking. Spotlights on a ceiling-mounted track can be used to throw direct light on to the pictures, or if you prefer a gentler, more diffuse light, choose uplights which throw light onto the ceiling from where it is reflected downward. It is also worth investigating new, low-voltage lighting systems which are far more flexible and less intrusive than conventional lighting.

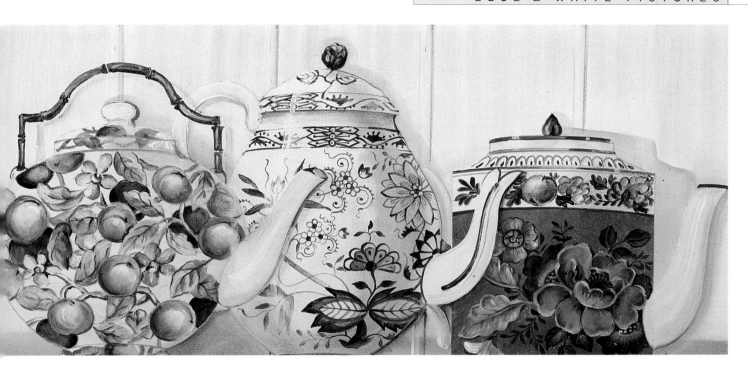

ABOVE LEFT AND BELOW LEFT
Galley, originally a ceramicist, meticulously researches her oil paintings of blue and white china. Her groups of teapots, tea caddies, or tea cups are bought with gusto by people wanting a strong blue and white painting. These works look especially striking when juxtaposed with actual pieces of china.

ABOVE Angelini's oil painting of three blue and white teapots on a shelf revels in intricate and bold fruit and flowers, beautiful against their white spouts. This painting would be perfect hung in a kitchen, perhaps over a plate rack full of real china.

RIGHT Aloe in a blue and white pot, from a series by Mary Kuper. Created in watercolor and gouache, this painting is inspired by a series painted in the eighteenth century by Weinmann.

155

SUPPLIERS

LEFT This whimsical oil painting by Monica Schaars shows the wild and domestic cat, who carries potted preserves while her natural quarry leap tantalizingly close. The print dress contrasts with the raw blue-grays of the sky.

AMERICA

All the big department stores are excellent sources of contemporary blue and white china, glass and linen, but there are also many other excellent sources that I recommend:

ANTIQUES

The American Wing
2415 Main Street
Bridgehampton, NY 11932
Tel: 516 537 3319

Amy Perlin Antiques
1020 Lexington Avenue
New York, NY 10021
Tel: 212 744 4923

English Country Antiques
Snake Hollow Road
Bridgehampton, NY 11932
Tel: 516 537 0606

Ruby Beets Antiques
Poxybogue Road
Bridgehampton, NY 14873
Tel: 516 537 2802

Sage Street Antiques
Sage Street
Sag Harbour, NY 11963
Tel: 516 725 4036

FABRICS AND TEXTILES

ABC Carpet & Home
881 Broadway, 5th Floor
New York, NY 10003
Tel: 212 473 3000

André Bon
979 Third Avenue
New York, NY 10022
Tel: 212 355 4012

Beacon Hill
979 Third Avenue
New York, NY 10022
Tel: 212 421 1200

Bennison Fabrics
76 Greene Street
New York, NY 10012
Tel: 212 941 1212

Calico Corners
203 Gale Lane
Kennett Square, PA 19348
Tel: 800 213 6366

Garnet Hill
Main Street
Franconia, NH 03580
Tel: 800 622 6216

Liberty of London
108 West 39th Street
New York NY 10018
Tel: 212 391 2150

Osborne & Little
979 Third Avenue
New York, NY 10022
Tel: 203 359 1500

Pierre Deux Fabrics
570 Madison Avenue
New York, NY 10021
Tel: 212 570 9343

Scalamandre Silk, Inc.
950 Third Avenue
New York, NY 10022
Tel: 212 980 9888

J. Schumacher & Company
79 Madison Avenue
New York, NY 10016
Tel: 212 213 7900

HOME FURNISHINGS

Bed, Bath & Beyond
Tel: 212 255 3550 for details

The Bombay Company
Tel: 800 829 7789 for details

Crate and Barrel
Tel: 847 272 2888 for details

Laura Ashley
Tel: 617 457 6000 for details

Portico Bed & Bath
139 Spring Street
New York, NY 10012
Tel: 212 941 7722

Pottery Barn
Tel: 800 922 5507 for details

Restoration Hardware
Tel: 415 924 8919 for details

Williams-Sonoma
Tel: 415 421 7900 for details

Wolfman Gold & Good Co.
117 Mercer Street
New York, NY 10012
Tel: 212 966 7055

PAINTS AND PAPERS

Kate's Paperie
561 Broadway
New York, NY 10012
Tel: 212 941 9816

Liberty Paint Company
969 Columbia Street
Hudson, NY 12534
Tel: 518 828 4060

Pearl Paint Company
308 Canal Street
New York, NY 10013
Tel: 212 431 7932

Sam Flax
12 West 20th Street
New York, NY 10001
Tel: 212 620 3038

Wolf Paints
Janovic Plaza
771 Ninth Avenue
New York NY 10019
Tel: 212 245 3241

UNITED KINGDOM
Blue and white china, glass,
linens, textiles and collectables
can be picked up in antique
shops, fairs and markets.

GOOD PLACES TO BROWSE
INCLUDE:

Alfie's Antiques Market
13–25 Church Street
London NW8 8DT
Tel: 0171 723 6066

Antiquarius
135 Kings Road
London SW3 4PW
Tel: 0171 351 5353

Camden Lock and The Stables
Chalk Farm Road
London NW1 8AH
Tel: 0171 485 5511

Camden Passage
339 Upper Street
London N1 0PB

Portobello Road Antiques Market
London W11

ANTIQUE CHINA

The Dining Room Shop
62 White Hart Lane
London SW13 0PZ
Tel: 0181 878 1020

Jonathan Horne
66c Kensington Church Street
London W8 4BY
Tel: 0171 221 5658

CONTEMPORARY CHINA
AND TABLEWARE

The Conran Shop
81 Fulham Road
London SW3 6RD
Tel: 0171 589 7401

Divertimenti
139 Fulham Road
London SW3 6SD
Tel: 0171 581 8065
and 45 Wigmore Street
London W1H 9LE
Tel: 0171 935 0639

General Trading Company
144 Sloane Street
London SW1X 9BL
Tel: 0171 730 0411

Habitat
Tel: 0171 255 2545 for details

Ikea
Tel: 0181 451 2767 for details

Jerry's Home Store
Tel: 0171 225 2246 for details

John Lewis Partnership
Tel: 0171 629 7711 for details

ANTIQUE GLASS

Guinevere Antiques
578 Kings Road
London SW6 2DY
Tel: 0171 736 2917

Jackdawes Antiques, at Fulham
Cross Antiques
320 Munster Road
London SW6 6BH

CONTEMPORARY GLASS

General Trading Company
– *see* Contemporary China and
Tableware

Habitat – *see* Contemporary
China and Tableware

Heal's
196 Tottenham Court Road
London W1P 9LD
Tel: 0171 636 1666

Jerry's Home Store – *see*
Contemporary China and
Tableware

William Yeoward
336 Kings Road
London SW3 5UR
Tel: 0171 351 5454

CONTEMPORARY FABRICS

Colefax & Fowler
110 Fulham Road
London SW3 6RL
Tel: 0171 244 7427

Designers Guild
267–277 Kings Road
London SW3 5EN
Tel: 0171 351 5775

Laura Ashley
Tel: 0171 736 6700 for details

Nobilis-Fontan
211 The Chambers
Chelsea Harbour
London SW10 0XF
Tel: 0171 351 7878

Pierre Frey
253 Fulham Road
London SW3 6HY
Tel: 0171 376 5599

Zimmer & Rohde
15 Chelsea Garden Market
Chelsea Harbour
London SW10 0XE
Tel: 0171 351 7115

CONTEMPORARY LINEN

Designers Guild– *see*
Contemporary Fabrics

Harrods
87 Brompton Road
Knightsbridge
London SW1X 7XL
Tel: 0171 730 1234

John Lewis Partnership – *see*
Contemporary China
and Tableware

Monogrammed Linen Shop
168 and 184 Walton Street
London SW3 2JL
Tel: 0171 589 4033 *and*
at Harvey Nichols
67 Brompton Road
London SW1X 7RG
Tel: 0171 225 2285 *or*
0171 235 5000

QUILTS

Anokhi Handworks
105 Kings Road
London SW3 4PA
Tel: 0171 376 3161

Chelsea Textiles
7 Walton Street
London SW3 2JD
Tel: 0171 584 1165

Damask
3&4 Broxholme House,
New Kings Road
London SW6 4AS
Tel: 0171 731 3553

The Indian Collection
4 Castle Street
Wallingford
Oxfordshire, OX10 8DL
Tel: 01491 833048 for stockists

The Java Cotton Company
3 Blenheim Crescent
London W11 2EE
Tel: 0171 229 3212

John Lewis Partnership – *see*
Contemporary China and
Tableware

Liberty
220 Regent Street
London W1R 6AH
Tel: 0171 734 1234

Valerie Wade
108 Fulham Road
London SW3 6HS
Tel: 0171 225 1414

BATHROOM FITTINGS

Colourwash
65 Fulham High Street
London SW6 3JJ
Tel: 0171 371 0911 *and*
125 Scrubbs Lane
London NW10 6QU
Tel: 0181 960 8983

Czech & Speake
125 Fulham Road
London SW3 6RT
Tel: 0171 225 3667

Pipe Dreams
70 Gloucester Road
London SW7 4QT
Tel: 0171 225 3978

Sitting Pretty
122 Dawes Road
London SW6 7EG
Tel: 0171 381 0049

ANTIQUE BATHS AND WCs

Drummonds of Bramley
Birtley Farm, Horsham Road
Surrey GU5 0LA
Tel: 01483 898 766

London Architectural Salvage
and Supply Company (LASSCO)
St Michaels's Church, Mark Street,
London EC2A 4ER
Tel: 0171 739 0448

The Water Monopoly
16 Longdale Road
London NW6 6RD
Tel: 0171 624 2636

INDEX

LEFT The heavy ornate gold of this urn implies weightiness, whereas the blue and white design in the center of the piece gives a sense of lightness, as if the scalloped gold were barely touching the porcelain.

alfresco dining 68–73

bathrooms 98–111, 158–159
bedrooms 77–97, 143, 145
blinds 58, 75, 79, 93, 100, 107
blue
    associations 7, 16, 53
    range 13, 27, 31, 36, 39, 137
    sources 14, 16
books 38, 121

candles 61, 75, 93, 131
Caribbean style 30, 54, 58, 70
china and porcelain
    bathrooms 99, 100, 104, 107, 108
    bedrooms 84–85
    collections 113–127
    dining rooms 8–11, 40–43, 58, 61,
        68, 75
    historic 14, 22, 122–126
    as inspiration 42
    kitchens 62–63, 65, 68
    in pictures 85, 119, 150–151,
        154–155
    sources 9, 156–157, 159
    white 131
Chinese pottery 14, 19, 40–44, 53,
    116–126, 159
cobalt blue 14, 126, 131
cool shades 36, 54, 58, 77, 88
cotton 36, 137, 140, 143

dark shades 39, 49
decorative objects 39, 87, 113–136,
    149, 158–159
dining rooms 8–9, 57–75, 117, 159

fabrics 137–143
    bathrooms 107, 111
    bedrooms 77–91
    dining areas 9, 60, 61, 73, 75
    kitchens 67, 68
    living areas 39, 50
    sources 157–158, 159
flowers 38, 50–51, 65, 71, 113, 114,
    144–151

glass 61, 62, 68, 102, 121, 131–135,
    157, 159

hallways 36, 52–53, 114
hutches 11, 60, 65, 68, 134

inspiration 31, 42, 55
Islamic art 14, 19, 22, 126

kitchens 60, 62–68, 130

light 46, 91, 93, 134, 154
linen 79–80, 100, 137, 138, 158
living rooms 33–55

markets 9, 79, 113, 156–157, 159
Mediterranean 27, 36, 46, 58, 108
mirrors 61, 91, 102, 134
monochrome approach 42, 50, 67

natural world 6, 13, 27, 77
neutral colours 55, 58

paint 16, 24, 31, 39, 46
pattern 39, 137–143
pictures 49, 82, 100, 111, 119, 145–155
pitchers 113, 114, 127

planning 24, 31, 42, 46, 55
plants 75, 114, 127, 148–150, 155
plate racks 68, 134
porcelain see china and porcelain

quilts 37, 77, 140, 158

rugs 34, 88, 107

shutters 35, 58, 87, 107
stencils 31, 39, 55
storage 62–63, 68, 96–97, 101, 134
sunrooms 57–59, 75
suppliers 156–159
Swedish style 16, 20, 42, 44, 55, 56, 58

tiles
    bathrooms 102–103
    dining rooms 58
    hallways 36, 52–53
    historic 14–15, 18, 22, 126, 128
    kitchens 64, 67, 73, 75, 130
    in pictures 153
    suppliers 158
toile 84, 94–96, 137, 140, 141, 143

vases 40, 60, 65, 84, 113, 114

wallcoverings 84, 88, 94–95, 107, 140
warm shades 55, 88